mer

THE
gremlins of
GRAMMAR

A Guide to Conquering the
Mischievous Myths That Plague
American English

Toni Boyle and K.D. Sullivan

McGraw·Hill

New York Chicago San Francisco Lisbon London Madrid Mexico City
Milan New Delhi San Juan Seoul Singapore Sydney Toronto

1 2 3 4 5 6 7 8 9 0   DOC/DOC   0 9 8 7 6 5

ISBN 0-07-145668-6

McGraw-Hill books are available at special quantity discounts to use as premiums and sales promotions, or for use in corporate training programs. For more information, please write to the Director of Special Sales, Professional Publishing, McGraw-Hill, Two Penn Plaza, New York, NY 10121-2298. Or contact your local bookstore.

This book is printed on acid-free paper.

*For Bill, who gave me so much, and for Cait,
who is a continuing gift*

—Toni

*For Mom, John, and Tawni . . . Thank you
for being my greatest fans!*

—K.D.

CONTENTS

ACKNOWLEDGMENTS

THIS BOOK WASN'T written in a vacuum. It's been a group effort, and I'm grateful to everyone whose input helped turn an idea into a reality. First, my gratitude to my coauthor, who was a driving force, as well as the perfect complement to everything we did, and to Karen Young and Craig Bolt, our brilliant editors at McGraw-Hill. Their keen eyes and illuminating insights filled in the spaces and improved the manuscript a thousandfold. Thanks to my parents, who preached grammar starting in the nursery; to the nuns at the Sacred Heart Academy, who drilled and reinforced the rules until they were second nature; and to Lyle Barnhart at Northwestern University, who taught me more about writing clearly than all my other writing instructors combined. I'm indebted to the long-suffering friends who listened to excerpts, offered suggestions, found examples, and kept me going in ways only they know—Richard Bates, Douglas Burns, Jim Cwik, Pam Daily, Dean Garrison, Diana Greenwood, Kurt Henschen, Sherry Mills, Susan RoAne, and Patricia Wiklund, along with so many others. And a special thank-you to my daughter, Caitlin, who's always behind my every endeavor, cheering me on and making me do better than I thought I could.

— Toni Boyle

Toni's right—we have many to thank, in our pasts and in our presents, for help with this book. My thanks to Toni, whose wit and humor are the center of this book. She's the one who did the "heavy lifting" of pulling this all together with such a fun, light touch. Also, some of the content is based on a series of job aids I put together for my business, with the great help of another excellent writer and collaborator, Merilee Eggleston. I echo Toni's thanks to our editor. Karen had such great input to help guide us. And she has the same sense of humor we do! And I thank Grace Freedson, my agent, who, I am happy to say, has been a supporter of mine for almost ten years now. I also owe a debt to the wonderful and talented people I have worked with over the years—and still do—whose dedication always inspires and motivates me.

Personal thanks go to my son John and my daughter-in-law Tawni for their support and love and for being proud of me—as I am of them. And my biggest thanks go to my

mom. She drove me crazy correcting my grammar when I was growing up. And, of course, I thank her for it immensely now. But even more than that, she is an incredible role model for me. She never finished high school, then as an adult she went back to school and got her Ph.D. By her words and her actions to this day, by her untiring support and encouragement of me, she continues to remind me that when you put your mind to something and work hard, limits exist only in your mind.

—K.D. SULLIVAN

INTRODUCTION

Wait!

Don't skip over this!

WE KNOW MOST people don't bother with the Introduction, but indulge us for a couple of pages. You may be thinking, "Oh, good, another grammar book—just what I've always wanted." We understand that. You'd think there were enough English language books out there to satisfy anyone's appetite for unintelligible rules and convoluted constructions—and there are. Shelves of them. We know. We've read a lot of them.

After our eyes uncrossed, we decided it was time to simplify the process, cut out the academic jargon, and, as Joe Friday used to say on *Dragnet*, "just give the facts, Ma'am."

We come at this from different perspectives. Toni had grammar drummed into her from her parents, from the nuns, and then in college and graduate school. K.D. had a less intense immersion, but her mother holds a Ph.D. in English and made sure things were said correctly at home. Toni is a professional writer and editor. K.D. is a writer and the proofreader's proofreader—she even wrote a book on the subject. Toni is less concerned with consistency than with style. K.D.—well, *anal* wouldn't be too strong. Together, we make a great team.

Both of us have a deep and abiding love of the language and an equally deep and abiding dislike for the pomposity that leads to incomprehensible rules and even less understandable applications. You may want to think of a verb as a *predicator*. We'd rather call it an *action word*. We don't talk about comma splices and fused sentences and appositives and all those other terms linguists and grammarians relish. Our goal is simplicity. We want you to understand what we're explaining, not be impressed because we can quote irrelevant rules.

What we aim to do is to give you a simple way to grasp what you need to know so you can write and speak English correctly. Our goal isn't to transform you into a Pulitzer Prize–winning writer or a nationally admired public speaker. We want to help those of you who, like us, sometimes stop and think, "Did I say that correctly?" or "That looks wrong." So much incorrect English is heard or seen in newspapers, television, radio, films, and books that it would be difficult not to be confused.

We're writing this in 2005, designated the Year of Languages in the United States. Wouldn't it be wonderful if one of the languages we all learned was our own? In the late 1970s, Toni was living in Chicago's Old Town neighborhood, where a language magnet school was being considered. This public school would teach ten or more languages to students drawn from all parts of the city. Looking for community support, a neighbor circulated a petition listing all the proposed languages. Toni questioned why English wasn't on the list. Said the neighbor, "English isn't a language. We all talk it." How much better if we could all speak it!

Within the next ten chapters, we'll take you on an adventure through our language—its separate pieces, the way those pieces connect, and finally how we use them in writing, on the Internet, and around the country.

We talk about each of the parts of speech and the punctuation that makes them come alive, whether they're shouting! or "conversing." Or pausing or stopping—or running on. And we finally sort out those poor misused pronouns—the *him* and *I* and *me* and *it* words that drive so many of us crazy. Verbs get the twice-over, with information you should know but don't have to remember, as well as a few basic rules you really must follow.

You find out the secrets for fixing vocabulary and spelling errors and how to "unconfuse" those word pairs that make us either "anxious" or "eager" to use them correctly. Once the toolbox is full, we show you how to build with the language and write with style, whether on paper or the Internet. We introduce you to global English and style sheets and business writing, sprinkled with a potpourri of the secret tricks of our trade and topped off with a killer list of books and websites that will take you through any grammar or writing crisis.

We also advise adherence to some structures, spellings, and usages that are now being accepted by a few authorities who have grown weary of fighting the tide of misuse and chosen to give in rather than stand their ground. You'll see several places where we acknowledge the change with the caveat that sometimes the original is better. Our job is to give you the map. We leave it to you to choose your verbal path.

We can guarantee the academic linguists and grammarians are going to be after us with interjections raised, howling in protest at our offhand attitude toward their sacred cows. Come and get us! While you're talking about predicates and past pluperfects, we'll be smiling indulgently and answering in words we can all understand.

Someone once said, "Genius is making the complex simple." (Toni contends, "Academic tenure is making the simple complex.") We're not geniuses, not by a long stretch, but we think we've taken the starch out of syntax and the gremlins out of grammar. If you agree, we've done our job.

Good English—whom cares? We do—and we hope you will, too.

GOOD ENGLISH — WHOM CARES?

HERE'S AN IDEA. Take a dictionary. Cut out all the words, and toss the tiny pieces of paper in the air as high as you can. When they fall to earth, try and make some sense of them. That's what it would be like if we tried to speak a language without grammar. Grammar gives us the form and the formulas that make random words turn into reasoned thoughts and structured sentences that logically and persuasively communicate thought.

Words and punctuation are like the separate pieces of a jigsaw puzzle. Alone, they're small bits of color, atoms in a universe. Assembled in the proper order, they're part of the large picture, each a vital keystone to the whole design. Just as matching puzzle pieces correctly reveals the picture, so grammar molds mere words into masterpieces.

In the sixteenth century, the French writer Montaigne wrote, "The majority of causes of trouble in this world are due to grammar." That may be a bit of an overstatement, but three hundred years later, American writer Mark Twain said about perfection in English grammar, "The thing just can't be done." Let's see if we can prove him wrong.

Before we get down to the nitty-gritty grammar gremlins, we want to spend a little time on the language itself. Ever thought about where American English came from? Why it breaks some stuffy old traditions, and how it's changing? That's what we'll be talking about in this chapter.

World English

We love facts, and these are pretty interesting, as facts go. Did you know . . .

* It's usually estimated that there are about 6,500 languages in the world. (We don't think that includes the six languages in the Star Trek universe: Vulcan, Romulan, Klingon, Bajoran, Ferengi, and Cardassian.)
* After Mandarin Chinese (more than a billion people chatter away in it), English is the most common language on the planet.
* There are probably about 300 million native English speakers, 300 million who consider it a second language, and another 100 million who use it as a foreign language.
* English is the official or co-official language of at least forty-five countries and is spoken extensively in countries where it has no official status. It's the language of science, aviation, computing, diplomacy, tourism, and increasingly, the Internet.

✳ Not a newcomer, English has been around since about 500 A.D., constantly changing and adapting and developing along the way.

Even if you're not as much of a word person as we are, it's fascinating to see how our language fits into the big picture and how it has held its own against the thousands of competitors.

Linguists are arguing, as they are wont to do, about what to call the English spoken in places other than the United States. In the 1920s, *World English* was understood to mean "standard English." Today, it's an encompassing term for Australian English, British English, Canadian English, Irish English, Nigerian English, and so on, each of which has its own twists and turns. Standard English definitely doesn't include the language those upstart rebels speak in the colonies. That would be *us*—or more properly, U.S.

It's interesting to notice that Canadian English is considered by linguists to be more closely allied to the British language than to ours. That's primarily because of spelling and vocabulary, which traditionally are more British. The influx of American television has begun to even out some of the distinctions, but spend time in Canada, read their newspapers, listen to their broadcasts, talk to the natives, and you'll quickly see and hear the sometimes slight but discernable differences, eh? It's more than just adding an extra *u* (*flavour, colour*) or ending words in *re* (*centre, theatre*) or saying "aboot" for *about* or ending sentences with "eh?" Canadian humorist and educator Stephen Leacock summed it up this way: "In Canada we have enough to do keeping up with two spoken languages [French and English] without trying to invent slang, so we just go right ahead and use English for literature, Scotch for sermons and American for conversation."

Heads Up 🌸

Reading British magazines is a good way to understand how subtle the deviations can be between American English and the British variety. Everything makes perfect sense—you are reading English after all—but somehow the gears don't mesh smoothly. It's a turn of phrase, a vocabulary word, an inflection that catches you up short and makes you realize you're not in Kansas anymore. We can understand each other in broad strokes. We're tripped up by the subtleties.

One of the most profound influences on the language was a man named Henry Fowler, who wrote *A Dictionary of Modern English Usage*, first published in 1926 and still in print. Twenty some years earlier, he wrote a composition manual for writers and journalists called *The King's English*. It immediately became the standard, and indeed, his five basic rules are as fresh as if they'd been written today.

* Prefer the familiar word to the far-fetched.
* Prefer the concrete to the abstract.
* Prefer the single word to the circumlocution.
* Prefer the short word to the long.
* Prefer the Saxon word to the Romance.

No argument there. However, it was also Mr. Fowler who came up with the mythical "don't split the infinitive" rule, which, as you'll see in Chapter 5, is wrong, wrong, wrong.

Ironically, as independent as we like to think ourselves, we still double-check with Britain just in case. It's like Dumbo holding a feather in his trunk so he could fly. We feel if we keep a "British feather" close at hand, we can be certain we're correct. That's why the *Oxford English Dictionary* is a standard reference and even has offices over here so it can be tuned into what those crazy Americans are saying now. The problem is that the two languages are different enough that the answers we get from "over there" may not be the correct answers over here. No one's right or wrong. We're just different.

Heads Up 🏵

If you're ever tempted to think that our language isn't so different from the rest of English, consider that translators at the European Union ask delegates if they want a translation to American or British English.

American English

When the Pilgrims came to Plymouth Rock, they brought their language with them. Once here, it began to grow and flourish. Even so, early British travelers to the colonies commented favorably on the "purity" of the English spoken in the New World. But that was before 1776, when the declaration of our independence waved our red, white, and blue flag in their faces. Our friends got a little hostile. Before long the rumors started that the Americans were ruining the English language. The rumors haven't stopped.

In 1995, 375 years after the *Mayflower* docked at Plymouth Rock, the Prince of Wales bemoaned the fate of English in America saying it was "very corrupting . . . people tend to invent all sorts of nouns and verbs and make words that shouldn't be." He then said he was going to try and maintain the "English English" superiority as a world language throughout the twenty-first century. At least it gives him something to do. You go, Charles! Since there are more than fifty dialects or regional accents in England, he has his work cut out for him.

Heads Up

Ever wonder why the British sound so proper and we sound so, well, American?

According to the experts, both sides have changed quite a bit, and, if anything, the accents of the south of England, which includes London, have changed more radically than have any American accents. The British accent we hear most often, according to linguists there, is that which people adopted if they wanted to better themselves in society. This is the accent of the educated speakers—think of the royal family, the prime minister, and the BBC broadcasters. Don't confuse it with the Cockney dialect from the East End, which is unintelligible even to many Londoners.

In the West Country of England, including Cornwall, Devon, and Somerset, the pace is slower and the natives speak very much the way we do in the southern United States, with a hint of a drawl. We don't interact with these British agricultural folk as often so we don't hear their similarity to us. Instead, we're most familiar with the accent of British politicians, comedians, and movie stars.

The plain fact is there are four to five times more American English speakers in the United States than there are British speakers in the United Kingdom, so we have a wider pool of people who are adding, subtracting, innovating, and revising the language as they go along. We're happy to report that most of them are totally oblivious to the changes—and the messes—they're making.

Perhaps the real problem with American English is that we don't learn it very well.

Changing English

If there's anything we should have learned by now, it's that the only thing that doesn't change is change. It's a constant. We have to change with it or be left in the dust. Language changes just like everything else. New words are added, old usages become dated. E. B. White wrote, "The living language is like a cow-path: it is the creation of the cows themselves, who, having created it, follow it or depart from it according to their whims or their needs. From daily use, the path undergoes change. A cow is under no obligation to stay."

American English has undergone major changes in the past century. Pick up a book written in 1905. You'll see how different the language is. It's more formal, more polite, more indirect. The teenager who a hundred years ago said, "I loathe and detest chemistry," now says, "Chemistry? Not!" In the twenty-first century, we speak out and up without giving a lot of thought to the effect our words are going to have. It's a "let it all hang out" philosophy that dominates our culture and permeates our speech.

Radio hosts, along with television and movie characters add words and phrases to the culture. Slang spikes the punch. The influx of immigrants from across the globe has brought new vitality to the language they're trying to learn. The old norms of perfect English are falling away.

In the hills of Tennessee, they still speak a form of Elizabethan English. The Pennsylvania Dutch speaker, who's really using a derivation of German-English, understands what you mean if you "throw your father out the window his hat." Minnewegian (Minnesota-Norwegian) is a subdialect spoken in northernmost Minnesota. Rent the movie *Fargo* to hear it. Don't forget California Surfer language—"gag me with a spoon"—and the Hawaiian pidgin English spoken on the sugar plantations. Louisiana has its Cajun English, with heavy borrowing from the French, and French Creole, which folds in the flavors of West Africa. And then there are the distinctive sounds of New York, Boston, and on up the coast.

Soon the pockets of dialect will be gone, and we'll be the poorer for it. The trick is to keep the regional flavors of American English while still reading and writing the language so we can all understand each other.

English Grammar

English and its grammar have never worried about being pristine pure. While it's a Germanic language, English borrows heavily from Latin and the romance languages of southern Europe. Like a potluck dinner, the invited and uninvited have dropped in and left a piece of their language on the table to be incorporated into the meal. Whatever wasn't left for us, we went out and took. In the 1800s, Booker T. Washington, then president of Tuskegee Institute, said, "We don't just borrow words; on occasion, English has pursued other languages down alleyways to beat them unconscious and rifle their pockets for new vocabulary."

This may partly explain why the spelling, pronunciation, and grammar rules are a collection of irregularities piled on irregularities. In what other language are you going to find a sentence like this?

Although the **bough** is **tough** wood, I'll saw **through** it.

Within the space of ten words, *ough* is pronounced four different ways. No wonder this language is such a nightmare to learn. Many feel that the discrepancies in pronunciation and spelling are a major reason English will never become the universal language. It's just too difficult. (Here's the good news—we already speak it, so we're a couple yards out in front of the pack.)

As we march through the first years of the twenty-first century, grammar appears doomed to be one of the lost arts. The media, written and broadcast, spew mistakes without the hint of an apology. On the other hand, we have the grim-faced academicians who can't accept that "the times they are a changing" and the language is going to change with them. The once sacrosanct grammar rules aren't so untouchable now. Mistakes are tolerated—well, not so much by us but by most people.

The issue becomes, is it better to say nothing than to say something incorrectly? Unless we want to become a nation of Harpo Marx clones, honking our horn instead of speaking up, then we vote for talking. Poor language skills are better than no language skills. If you've ever learned a foreign language, you know the hardest thing in the world to do is test your skills on a native speaker. But if you stay quiet, you'll never become more fluent. Mistakes are part of the process.

Here's the point: whether or not you write or speak "classic English" well, if the person you're communicating with doesn't understand you, it's an exercise in futility. This doesn't mean you can throw away all the rules, but it does mean there are some you don't have to worry about. We're in favor of scrubbing terms like *pluperfect past participle* from the grammar guides and sticking to the basics. The rules and regulations we'll be talking about are the necessary ones, those that give American English its subtlety and spice as it morphs into a new language reflecting the diversity of the United States.

Take what you need from the buffet we're about to lay in front of you—a nibble here, a bite there—until your plate is full. Don't sweat the nitty-gritty. Loosen up and laugh. This is a language after all, not nuclear science.

Five Major Facts About English and Grammar

Some of our favorite facts:

* Of the 6,500 languages in the world, English is the second most spoken after Mandarin Chinese.
* English may never become the universal language because of the difficulty of its vocabulary and pronunciation.
* One of the biggest challenges in American English is that most Americans don't speak it very well.
* Mark Twain said of perfection in English grammar, "The thing just can't be done."
* Enjoy yourself. English is a language, not brain surgery.

COVERING THE BASICS, PART ONE

Parts of Speech

BEFORE WE CAN begin to talk about grammar, we've got to introduce you to the individual parts of speech that grammar works with. Each one is important, even those we don't use very often. Once upon a time we all learned these words, complete with fancy names and unintelligible rules. Now we'll give you the real scoop, cutting out the forgettable "grammarspeak" and only telling you what you really need to know. Again, we warn the strict grammarians that some of what we say may cause them to break out in hives. To us, the beauty and challenge of the language is its versatility, which often leaves usage rules open to interpretation.

We wish we could promise you'd never have to learn anything more than nouns and verbs, but the English language is a bit more complicated than that. What we do promise is that you won't have to be bothered with anything that isn't essential. To the dismay of ardent grammarians, we won't be discussing the more intricate subtleties of grammar and usage. This is not a grammar book. It's not even a style manual in the strictest sense of the term.

Toni's Tidbits

In the 1960s I interviewed Charles Berlitz, writer and member of the world-famous language school family, for a radio show I hosted in Detroit. At that time, he spoke more than forty languages and had invented a couple of his own. He told me that of the world's major languages—except for the challenges of learning a totally different alphabet, like Chinese ideographs, Cyrillic, or Arabic characters, or the African Bushman click language (Xhosa)—English was by far the most difficult to speak and write correctly. It draws from so many other languages for vocabulary and style and has so many irregularities and contradictions in usage that it's almost impossible for anyone but the most hard-nosed grammar maven to be correct 100 percent of the time. That's good news for those of us who make our living with the language—but no excuse for not trying to do it justice. So let's take it one step at a time and make passably perfect English as painless as possible.

First and foremost, you need at least a nodding acquaintance with the basic parts of speech. Pretty hard to construct a building if you can't tell the difference between a brick and a buzz saw. In the same way, you can't construct a sentence if you don't recognize the difference between nouns and verbs, adjectives and adverbs, prepositions and conjunctions. So let's take a few minutes, go back to the elementary school classroom, and brush up on some old lessons. Some of this you need to remember. A lot of it you can read and relegate to the back burner.

Nouns

All together now: "a noun is the name of a person, place, or thing." That wasn't so hard. A noun is either the subject or object of the sentence. In other words, it's the person doing (subject) or being done to (object). This makes more sense when we get to verbs.

Nouns come in three basic genders: masculine, feminine, and neuter. We only have to worry about this if we're using a pronoun, a word standing in for or referring back to a noun.

Nero Wolfe, **he** was the detective, gave Trixiebelle, **she** was his client, a homegrown orchid, **it** was his favorite.

Females are referred to as *she* or *her*, males as *he* or *him*, and genderless nouns as *it*. By tradition, a few neuter nouns have been given a gender through usage. For instance, ships and airplanes are usually referred to as *she*. This might be because at one time, only men commanded them, but let's not go there.

Heads Up 🍁

While English doesn't assign a gender to every noun, we would be remiss if we didn't mention the current trend toward deleting any nuance of sexism. To make certain no person feels discriminated against, many gender-specific words have been neutralized. *Waiters* and *waitresses* have been replaced by *servers*. *Postmen* have become *mail carriers*, *firemen* are now *firefighters*, and *stewardesses* have become *flight attendants*. This has extended to less specific words as well. *Mankind* is *humankind*, yesterday's *old wives' tale* is today's *superstition*, and your *forefather* is now your *ancestor*. Whatever. To us, it's a bit of overkill, but be aware that we may be in the minority. In this case, if you want to be safe and not pelted with rotten tomatoes by the Political Correctness Police, choose to be neutral.

Pronouns

We've devoted all of Chapter 4 to pronouns, which are nothing more than little words that stand in for nouns (and cause a great deal of commotion in the process), so we're not going to spend much time on them here.

Why do we make such a fuss about pronouns? Simple. They are the most sinned against of all the parts of speech. *I*, *me*, *he*, *him*, *she*, *her*, and all the pronoun variations seem to have been lost in the shuffle. Amazingly, even the best spoken among us will occasionally blurt out a sentence that makes you wince—or should.

Me and the team are meeting Mr. Trump in the boardroom.

Should be: The team and **I** are meeting Mr. Trump in the boardroom.

David and **her** are going to hear "You're fired!"

Should be: **She** and David are going to hear "You're fired!"

Anyone who thought, even for a heartbeat, that the first and third examples were correct doesn't deserve to be an apprentice! Go directly to Chapter 4, and don't come back until you've got it figured out.

Adjectives

The job of an adjective is to tell you more about the noun it modifies. The purists will tell you there are four kinds of adjectives: descriptive, proper, limiting, and predicate.

Descriptive adjectives describe the noun in terms of its kind, color, shape, size, etc.—the *witty* wordsmith, the *rotund* diva, the *puce* pantaloons, the *passionate* purveyor, the *magnificent* obsession.

Proper adjectives are descriptive adjectives derived from proper nouns. The only trick here is to remember that proper adjectives require a capital letter. Think of *French* fries, *English* muffins, *Indian* summer, *Italian* flag, *Brussels* sprouts, *Canadian* bacon, *Dutch* treat, *American* cheese, and a host of others.

Limiting adjectives describe the noun in terms of how many, how much, which one, whose, etc.—We *three* kings shared a *single* throne with much discomfort. Two limiting words we rarely think to put in the adjective column are *a* (*an*) and *the*. Any one of the *three* tells you that it is only *one* we're talking about.

Sometimes English is said to be less precise than other languages, but *a* and *the* can be very defining. The distinction was made very clear in 2002 when the wedding of two opera singers was announced in *The New York Times*. The bride was referred to as *a soprano* (one of many), while the better-known groom was identified as *the bass* (defining the group). They did it again when they announced that *the chef* Bobby Flay married *an actress*, Stephanie March. Let's hope the newspaper's ranking of talent didn't turn the reception into a sour note or send the honeymoon up in flames.

Predicate adjectives have a dual function. They modify the noun, but they also complete the verb. They always directly follow the linking verb. *Is, grow, look, smell, prove, keep, seem, become, appear*, etc., are typical linking verbs.

"This television show **is *stupid*,**" said Donald, forgetting he'd produced it.

Jack and his beanstalk **grew *tall***, but the giant **grew *taller***.

"Something **is *rotten***️ in the state of Denmark." (*Hamlet*)

Nothing really difficult about any of that, but there is one peril in the adjective pot: comparisons. Often it's not enough to describe the noun without making sure everyone knows it's vastly superior to all others in its category. These comparison adjectives are divided into positive (*fine*), comparative (*finer*), and superlative (*finest*).

Susie, a **sadder** but **wiser** gal, gave back the ring.

Your ten-year-old may be at Harvard, but my ten-year-old is the **brightest** in her kindergarten class.

Toni's personal favorite is an illustration by cartoonist Sandra Boynton in which a turkey announces, "I'm eruditer than you."

Not much of a challenge. Basically, when you want to say "a little bit more than average," add *-er* to the word. When you mean the top of the line, there's no equal, add *-est*. Right? Not quite. Some words don't lend themselves to these endings, so you have to modify them with *more* or *most*.

Without a single face card, it was **more advantageous** to retreat.

Rex was the **most admired** man on the planet, or so he thought.

Heads Up 🔆

Time for a couple of rules. One-syllable adjectives usually take *-er* or *-est*: *meaner, swifter, keenest, leanest*, etc. Adjectives consisting of two or more syllables take *more* or *most*, unless they end in *-y*. Then you can lop off the *-y* and add *-ier* or *-iest*. Think *sillier, handier, busier, sexiest, clumsiest, shadiest*, etc.

One of the challenges of English is that there are dozens of exceptions to most rules, and you just have to learn them. In fairness, they exist in other languages, too, but we aren't concerned here with the odd conjugation of certain French verbs or the nonagreement of some gender-specific Italian nouns. There are at least six—and probably more—comparative adjectives we use every day that don't follow the rules just cited. Recognize them and you'll be fine.

Heads Up ✦

IRREGULAR COMPARISON OF ADJECTIVES

Positive	Comparative	Superlative
bad	worse	worst
far	farther/further*	farthest/furthest
good/well	better	best
little	less	least
many/much	more	most
out	outer	outermost/ utmost

* In Chapter 6 we discuss the difference between *farther* and *further*. (Yes, there is a difference.)

There's one last thing to point out about adjectives. Some adjectives should never be compared, but we do it all the time anyway. Words like *perfect, unique, incomparable, full, fatal, universal, ultimate, final,* etc., say it all. Just like you can't be *somewhat pregnant,* you can't be *more perfect.* Some words express the superlative without any fussing on our part. So avoid the temptation to describe the *most incomparable* date you've ever had. If it's incomparable, there's nothing to compare with it, so don't.

Verbs

Verbs are action words. They tell the subject (noun or pronoun) of the sentence what to do and explain what's being done to the object (noun or pronoun).

Verbs come in various forms. They are transitive or intransitive or both. They are regular or irregular. Some are auxiliary verbs, which are those that help the main verb express its meaning. We spend all of Chapter 5 talking about verbs. We can hear your heart beating faster.

Adverbs

Nouns have adjectives, and, not to be one-upped, verbs have adverbs. These are words that add specificity to the verb as well as to other words—as long as they're not nouns or pronouns. Adverbs can show time (*often, rarely, occasionally, constantly*), manner (*breathlessly, eagerly, shamelessly, catastrophically*), degree (*very, less, more, extremely*), or place (*here, there, everywhere, nowhere*).

Adverbs even modify adjectives.

Who knew the ***strikingly*** **handsome** prince started out as a frog?

The ***dramatically*** **daffy** diva didn't delay the deposition.

Most of the rules governing adverbs are pretty straightforward. There are technicalities, such as adverbial clauses that start with words like *because* or *so* or *although*, but again we're getting into the province of the grammarians, and that's not our planned destination.

K.D.'s Proofreading Perspective ✴

When a compound modifier contains an adverb that ends in
-*ly*, the two words are *never* hyphenated. Sounds complicated,
but it's not. You see it all the time. Even though you may think
these words are begging to be together, don't give in.

▌He's a *highly* **motivated** Internet researcher, though unfortunately for his eyes and back, not an *easily* **distracted** one.

Prepositions

Prepositions are those little words that show us the relationship between nouns or noun substitutes. They come in
two varieties, simple and complex, and they are always followed by a noun. The result is what's called a *prepositional
phrase*.

> The ogre hid out **under the bridge**.

> **Beneath the lily pad**, the frog waited for a princess
> to kiss him.

> **For richer** or **for poorer, in sickness** and **in
> health** . . .

The most common simple prepositions are

about	across
above	after

against	inside
along	into
among	near
around	of
at	off
before	on
behind	since
below	through
beneath	to
beside	toward
between	under
beyond	until
by	up
during	upon
except	with
for	within
from	without
in	

Complex prepositions combine two or three words to act as one preposition: *according to, insofar as, instead of, along with*. All you have to remember is that they, too, require a subject.

Many card games are played ***according to* Hoyle**.

***Instead of* the typical response**, Jeremy chose to answer in Sanskrit.

Tonight's performance is cancelled ***due to* illness**; last night it made the critics sick.

While prepositions aren't one of the major migraines in English, they do present a few issues. For little words, they can

be misused in a big way. A few of the most obvious victims
are *in/at*, *from/than*, *among/between*, and *in/into*. Let's clear
up the confusion right now.

* **In or at?** Use *in* with spaces (*in* the universe, *in* the
bath, *in* a row, *in* a field of study). Use *at* with places (*at* the
resort, *at* the top of the page, *at* the back of the room).
Therefore,

> Although I sat **at the front** of the classroom **in col-
> lege**, I was still bad **in math**.

* **From or *than*?** This one is easy. It should always be *different from*. The commonly heard *different than* is only used
in American English, and it's always incorrect. (Besides,
than isn't a preposition. It's a conjunction. We rest our case.)
Therefore,

> Even more **than** I thought, rugby is **different from**
> baseball.

* **Among or *between*?** Usually, *among* is used when more
than two parties or things are involved. *Between* is preferred
when there are only two. Ergo,

> Smaller prizes were divided **among** the participants,
> while the big money was split **between** the two
> winners.

However, from its earliest usage, *between* has been extended
to more than two, for instance,

> There were varying positions on the treaty **between**
> Timbuktu, Tasmania, and Turkey.

In common usage, either *among* or *between* is correct. Just listen for the sense of the sentence.

✳ ***In* or *into*?** In many instances, either one is correct, or the correct choice is obvious. *Into* implies an action, while *in* most often describes a condition. For instance,

> Lassie jumped **in/into** the lake to save Timmy from the alligator.
>
> While skiing **in** Switzerland, I fell **into/in** a snow bank.

Heads Up ✳

You've undoubtedly figured out by now that we take special delight in tweaking the noses of prudish grammarians. Well, here's another carved-in-stone rule that can be broken because it never existed. It is perfectly permissible to end a sentence with a preposition. That's right! Convoluting sentence structure so the preposition doesn't land at the end is an exercise in futility we no longer have to deal with.

In checking sources, we found the following anecdote may or may not have been accurately attributed to the former British prime minister Sir Winston Churchill. It seems the crusty gentleman was very proud of his English writing style. When an editor handed back a manuscript in which a sentence had been rearranged to rectify a dangling preposition, Sir Winston was reported to have replied, "This is the sort of English up with which I will not put." That explains it as well as anything else we've heard, no matter who actually said it.

Conjunctions

Conjunctions are such nice words—and there are so few of them. Conjunctions connect ideas. Some are coordinating—*and, but, or, nor, for, so, yet*—connecting words, phrases, or clauses of equal rank.

> **Nick *and* Nora** solved the crime, with Asta's help, of course.

> **Not one *but* two** amaryllis bloomed on a single stalk.

Other conjunctions are subordinating—*after, because, if, since, when, where, while*—connecting subordinate clauses. A subordinate clause replaces a noun, an adjective, or an adverb because it can't stand alone.

> *While Victoria was queen*, England took the moral high road.

One of the nicest aspects of conjunctions is you can't get in much trouble with them. We like that.

Interjections

The last part of speech is equally simple. We mention it because perhaps you didn't know it had a name. Interjections are words like *ouch, oops, oh, yikes, horrors, aha*, etc. The newest interjection added to the dictionary is Homer Simpson's *doh!*, which made it into the updated online edition of the *Oxford English Dictionary* in 2001. These are words that express a strong emotion or feeling. They may be followed by a comma, but more commonly interjections are followed by an exclamation point.

Oh, I'm so sorry I didn't see you sitting there.

Horrors! The mice are marching on the cabinet in formation.

Ouch! Haven't you ever heard of anesthetic, Doc?

The most important rule to remember about interjections is not to overuse them. They are like jalapeño peppers. A taste is fine. A whole plate makes your eyes water.

Heads Up

Now that you can recognize all the parts of speech, realize that the wonderful flexibility of English allows the same word to be used in any number of ways.

▌"You call that **running**? I've seen babies crawl faster," the coach snarled. (noun)

▌To avoid error, the scorekeepers kept a **running** tally. (adjective)

▌The cheetah **was running** faster than any of the zebras it was chasing. (verb)

▌The thief left the bank **running** but tripped and fell over the curb. (adverb)

Relish the myriad ways to use words to keep your language fresh.

Ten Parts of Speech Rules You Have to Know 🦟

OK, we assume that you have absorbed everything in this chapter and now know as much as anyone would ever want to know about the parts of speech. However, just in case you need a little crutch to lean on from time to time, here are the bare-bones facts:

1. Nouns name a person, place, or thing and are either masculine, feminine, or neuter.
2. Pronouns take the place of or refer back to nouns.
3. Adjectives come in four varieties: descriptive, proper, limiting, and predicative.
4. Comparative adjectives—*nice, nicer, nicest*—can be irregular—*good, better, best.*
5. Verbs are action words that can be regular—*wash, washed, washed*—or irregular—*write, wrote, written.*
6. Verbs and nouns must agree if the sentence is to make sense.
7. Adverbs can modify verbs or adjectives and add the missing specifics.
8. Prepositions, which can end a sentence, show the relationship *between* nouns or noun substitutes *in* one way or another.
9. Conjunctions connect one idea to another *and* do it well.
10. Interjections are usually followed by an exclamation point and should be used sparingly so they don't lose their impact.

3

COVERING THE BASICS, PART TWO

Punctuation Marks

IN CHAPTER 2 WE SAID you needed to know a brick from a buzz saw if you were going to construct a building. In this chapter we're going to discuss what goes between those bricks so their layout makes sense.

Punctuation may seem like a no-brainer, but whole books have been devoted to where commas belong and how to properly insert apostrophes. Obviously, none of these books is working because mistakes are still rampant. It's hard to get through a day without seeing where someone has had a total disregard for the placement of these little marks.

Let's look at each one individually.

The Period (.)

We call that tiny bit of ink at the end of a sentence a *period*. The British, still under the assumption that English is their language, call this essential flyspeck a *full stop*. Telegrams—remember them?—shortened that to *stop*.

> Dear Mom **Stop** College great **Stop** Send money **Stop**

(Maybe that should be *don't stop!*)

The Internet world discarded the word *period* altogether, referring to it as *dot*. You'd pronounce http://www.TrustUs.com as "http colon slash slash w w w *dot* TrustUs *dot* com."

The basic job of the period is to point out where the sentence ends and your voice should drop if you're reading aloud. But it's so much more versatile than that.

Periods also follow most abbreviations to indicate that the word has been shortened.

> **Mrs.** Throckmorton, a Harvard **M.B.A.**, didn't **R.S.V.P.** to the 7 P.M. dinner invitation.

However, usage has changed in this world of acronyms, where the first initials of words are often combined to make a new word, like NATO (North Atlantic Treaty Organisation), JPEG (Joint Photographic Experts Group), scuba (Self-Contained Underwater Breathing Apparatus), or James Bond's nemesis, SPECTRE (Special Executive for Counterintelligence, Terrorism, Revenge, and Extortion). In these cases, we drop the periods between the letters.

When the first letters of the organization can't be pronounced as a word, it's called an *initialism*. We used to write the periods between the letters, but today they are more commonly omitted, as in ASPCA (American Society for the Prevention of Cruelty to Animals), the YMCA (Young Men's Christian Association), SPEBSQSA (Society for the Preservation and Encouragement of Barber Shop Quartet Singing in America), or one of the Web's many contributions to the acronym vocabulary, HTML (HyperText Markup Language).

ADCOMSUBORDCOMPHIBSPAC is usually awarded the dubious honor of being the longest acronym in English. It is the brainchild of the U.S. Navy and stands for Administrative Command, Amphibious Forces, Pacific Fleet Subordinate Command. We're not sure how our sailors came up with this acronym or why it's an improvement on the original full-word designation, but you can't say we didn't tell you about it. It might win you a trivia contest someday.

The best way to know if an acronym does or doesn't take periods between the letters is to consult the most current edition of a good dictionary.

K.D.'s Proofreading Perspective ✦

For those of us who sit at a computer much of the day and don't always want to take the time to walk all the way over to the bookcase, Acronym Finder (acronymfinder.com) is a great resource (there are more in the Appendix) for finding definitions in seconds for almost any acronym, abbreviation, or initialism. It's a terrific tool that lets you sort by category and industry.

Heads Up 🔅

When a sentence ends with an abbreviation that has a period, you don't need to put in another period. For instance,

▌ After midnight, Cinderella will lose the coach, footmen, fancy clothes, etc.

When typing on a computer—and how else do we type these days?—you don't have to double-space after a period. The computer does the formatting for you. We can always tell an author of our generations because the manuscript invariably arrives with a double-space after each period. Please retrain yourself! It will save your editors so much wear and tear on the delete key as they remove those extra spaces.

The Comma (,)

Commas are periods with a little tail that indicate where to pause in a sentence and that add clarity to what you're saying. Like most things, too few can result in chaos and too many can be equally confusing.

Toni's Tidbits 🔅

K.D. Sullivan and I are good friends, as well as professional colleagues, but we have radically different viewpoints on the comma. Much of my background is in spoken-word audio, in which the announcer is cued when to breathe and how to phrase by the insertion of commas in the script. As a result— and because I learned my early lessons from teachers who revered the comma—I tend to strew them liberally, like Gretel bouncing down the forest path toward the wicked witch, leaving a trail of bread crumbs behind to guide her home.

K.D., the eagle-eyed editor, swoops behind me picking up 75 percent of the comma crumbs and whisking them away. She undoubtedly has a huge barrel of my commas in a corner of her yard, but I have an even larger reserve in the back of my desk drawer.

Unfortunately, she is usually correct, but that doesn't mean I'm going to change anytime soon, especially because I have the comfort of knowing she's there to clean up after me.

(Note from K.D.: Don't tell Toni, but those commas of hers are part of a landfill project near the Golden Gate Bridge. Actually, she's contributing so much they may give her a plaque.)

Here are the basic rules—and the irregularities (or *howevers*)—to remember:

✳ Commas are used to separate items in a series, including before the final *and* or *or*. This is correctly termed a *series* (or *serial*) *comma*, and its function is to clarify a list of things or people—or ducks.

The Disney studios gave us Donald, Daisy, Huey, Dewey, and Louie Duck.

However, don't use a comma if an ampersand (&) replaces the final *and*.

Dewey, Cheatem & Howe was the best legal firm in town.

* Commas separate adjectives before a noun if you could replace the comma with *and*.

> Scarlett, the most **beautiful, flirtatious** girl at the party, went home alone.

However, don't use a comma if one adjective modifies the other.

> Her **flaming red** hair signaled a temper just as incendiary.

* Commas signal a natural pause.

> Yes indeed, Scarlett will give Rhett more trouble than he bargained for.

However, don't use a comma between the opening phrase and the verb it modifies.

> Right behind Mother Hubbard came all her children.

* Commas usually precede any of the seven connecting conjunctions: *and, but, for, or, nor, so,* and *yet*.

> The story, and I swear it's true, sounds more like fiction than fact.

However, don't use a comma when two or more verbs have the same subject, unless, of course, omitting it would cause confusion—but you knew that, right?

> Cinderella rode to the ball and danced all night with the prince.

Cinderella rode to the ball and danced all night with the prince, remembering to leave at midnight.

✳ Commas set off extraneous information. As you can see, if you take out the material between the commas, these sentences still make sense, although they're not as complete or interesting.

The prince, an only child with indulgent parents, fell in love immediately.

The prince fell in love immediately.

The love of his life, Cinderella, left as mysteriously as she had arrived.

The love of his life left as mysteriously as she had arrived.

However, don't use a comma if you have two thoughts that aren't connected by *or*, *and*, or *but*. Technically, this structure takes a semicolon, which we address later in the chapter.

✳ Commas separate introductory clauses that set the scene and begin with words like *after*, *although*, *as*, *because*, *if*, *since*, *when*, *while*, etc.

While the dwarfs were at work, Snow White cleaned the cottage.

However, if the introductory phrase or clause is very short, the comma may be omitted.

By Friday the cottage was sparkling, and Snow White had the weekend to herself.

* Commas are used to set off elements of a place-name or an address.

> The Disney Studios are in Burbank, California, not in Hollywood.

However, they don't separate months and years unless a specific date is mentioned.

> Instead of a June 2006 wedding, Cinderella and the prince will marry on November 9, 2006, in the palace chapel.

* Commas are used in names that incorporate Jr., Sr., II, III, Inc., Ltd., etc.

> Reginald P. Snerdly, Jr., works for Snerdly Enterprises, Ltd.

However, they don't have to be used in that instance. It's your call.

> Reginald P. Snerdly Jr. works for Snerdly Enterprises Ltd.

Had enough of commas? The most important rule to remember is that they must add sense or shading to the sentence. They should be used when *not* using them makes it difficult to understand the meaning. Or you can be like Toni and sprinkle them everywhere and hope K.D. comes along behind you to make things right.

K.D.'s Proofreading Perspective

This is a rule in *The Chicago Manual of Style*—to use the *serial comma*, as it's called (though I prefer the term *series comma*). However, a lot of people (like someone I know with whom I'm coauthoring a book) and also, in fairness, *The Associated Press Stylebook* don't use them, and that can also be an accepted style—as long as you're consistent in your use.

The Semicolon (;)

What do you get when you combine a comma and a period? Right! A semicolon. And it actually makes some sense that the semicolon is made up of these two punctuation marks because they combine two thoughts of equal rank. Often the thoughts separated by a semicolon could be divided into two sentences, but that's a matter of style more than grammar.

A semicolon has been called a *weak period*, and we have to admit it's not one of our favorite punctuation marks because of that. But you are going to come across it, and you should know when to use it. Here are a couple of examples:

The Wizard of Oz didn't stop the wind; even he couldn't control a tornado.

Little Miss Muffet sat on a tuffet; the spider hung on a thread by her head.

We could also tell you that semicolons separate main clauses when they're not connected by a coordinating conjunction in compound complex sentences, but we're not sure that rule does anyone any good—and no one is going to know what it means. Just use semicolons the way we just indicated, and you'll be fine. When in doubt, split the thought into two sentences. Whatever you do, use semicolons sparingly.

K.D.'s Proofreading Perspective 🎇

Here's one time when a semicolon is actually *required*: when there's a series of items that include "internal" commas. For example,

▌ She had lived in Honolulu, Hawaii; Paris, France; and New York, New York, before settling in San Francisco, California.

The Colon (:)

This is another compound punctuation mark. The colon is actually two periods, one piled on top of the other. If the semicolon is a weak period, the colon is a strong stop.

Unlike the semicolon, which separates equal parts of a sentence, the colon is used to introduce a thought that follows.

Here's what little boys are made of: snips and snails and puppy dog tails.

The following characters all showed up in threes: the little pigs, the mittenless kittens, and the billy goats gruff.

A colon can also separate two parts of the sentence when the second part further explains the first.

Little Red Riding Hood had a heart of gold: her grandmother didn't live to see it.

As you've probably gathered, the colon can be replaced by the em dash—so named because it is the width of the letter *m*—in casual English, which is the language most of us speak and write in today's Internet-intensive culture. (Toni tends to like the em dash almost as well as she likes commas and has made K.D. a convert.)

Here are two other points to remember: (1) today, most stylebooks do not call for a capital first letter after a colon even if what follows is a full sentence, and (2) like the period, only one space follows a colon.

K.D.'s Proofreading Perspective ✳

When using an em dash, it's a matter of choice whether you put a space before and after it — like this, or not—like this. Whichever style you choose, be consistent each time it is used.

Of course, the four most obvious uses of the colon are these:

✳ In business correspondence after *Dear Sir:* or the ever so warm and fuzzy *To Whom It May Concern:*
✳ In telling time, to separate the hours and minutes, as in 12:30

✳ When referring to biblical chapter and verse, as in Ecclesiastes 10:19

✳ Between the title and subtitle of a book, as in *Painful Prose: How to Write Bad English the First Time and Every Time*

Don't overuse the colon. You and your reader will be happier that way.

The Ellipsis (. . .)

As long as we're talking about period-related punctuation, let's not forget the ellipsis. Made up of three periods in a row, the ellipsis indicates something is missing. Check your local paper's movie listings, especially for movies that the critics panned, or look at ads for books or music albums. The companies often quote reviews in order to hype their offering. You'll find the ellipsis lives where the review most needs editing to appear positive.

An ad for a kids' movie quoted a review, but not in its entirety:

"Mystery Inc. does it again . . . this time better than ever."

An ad for the paperback edition of a book featured these three quotes:

"Gorgeous . . . historically rich . . . intricately surprising." (*New York Daily News*)

"Poignant . . . remarkable." (*Washington Post Book World*)

"Arresting . . . gripping." (*Publishers Weekly*)

The ellipsis takes out all the extraneous verbiage, including any that might not be so positive, and shows you that the material has been edited.

You can also use the ellipsis to take out part of a text that is too long or not germane.

"Once upon a time there was a princess . . . and they lived happily ever after."

Increasingly, we see the ellipsis used as a dash—or even a pause between thoughts. This is especially common in e-mails. Who knows? Thirty years from now someone may write a book saying, "Remember when they thought you couldn't use the ellipsis this way?" Language changes. Rules change. Comfort levels change. But for right now, you're clued in to what's correct.

K.D.'s Proofreading Perspective

The ellipsis (or if you're using more than one, ellipses) doesn't play well with others, so always leave one space on either side of it and the words or punctuation next to it. If the omitted material comes after the end of a sentence, leave one space after the period.

▌ The prince and his bride lived happily ever after. . . .

If the omitted material comes before the end of the sentence, it's ellipsis-space-period (or whatever punctuation is called for).

▌ The prince and his bride lived happily . . . .

> We know it looks strange and not all style guides agree, but use it as we've shown and you'll be fine. Better yet, try not to use the ellipsis at the end of a sentence.

The Apostrophe (')

Nothing but a superscript comma, the apostrophe seems to have everyone scurrying about trying to decipher where it goes and what difference it makes. Actually, it makes a humungous difference. How you use the apostrophe can get you in almost as much trouble as how you use pronouns. Bestsellers have focused on its use, misuse, or omission. The British have a society dedicated to its protection, while British writer and columnist Keith Waterhouse has anointed himself president for life of the Association for the Annihilation of the Aberrant Apostrophe.

It can all seem a bit overwhelming. The good news is you only have to remember three primary instances in which the apostrophe is used. A short list, but an important one.

✳ The A-Number-One Rule guiding the use of apostrophes is that they are to show possession, not plurality. When you put -'s on the end of a noun, it indicates ownership.

> **The attorneys** (plural) watching out for **Little Red Riding Hood's** (possessive) **interests** (plural) denied being paid by the **wolf's** (possessive) family.

That being said, we are now going to contradict this rule in just this one instance—the ever-popular pronoun *it*.

When you refer to *it's teeth*—still talking about the wolf, of course—what you've said is *it is teeth*. *It's* is a contraction of the verb *it is* (or sometimes *it was*). In this one case, the possessive does not use the apostrophe and is *its*. This pronoun seems to be so confusing that we talk about it again in Chapter 6, where it's included with our Fifty Sets of Commonly Confused Words.

Its teeth were huge, so **it's** a good thing the hunter had a gun.

We know we've said this before and we'll say it again because it's misused so often. We're determined you'll know the difference between *its* and *it's* by the time you've finished reading this book.

✳ The apostrophe is used to show that letters have been omitted, for instance in verb contractions—*can't* (cannot), *didn't* (did not), *couldn't* (could not), *he's* (he is), *you're* (you are), *we'll* (we will), etc. It's also used when numbers are missing—the '60s (1960s).

K.D.'s Proofreading Perspective ✳

If you're using curly apostrophes as opposed to straight ones, when you want an apostrophe like in "the '60s," be sure the apostrophe is facing the right way—as a true apostrophe, not an opening single quotation mark. In typing on a computer, how do you achieve that? Type both an opening and a closing single quotation mark, and then delete the opening one.

✳ After a lowercase letter, you should use -'s to indicate more than one, especially if you're minding your *p's and q's*. This is probably more for clarity on the typed page than to satisfy a grammar rule. However, if the letters are capitalized, no apostrophe is needed to show plurals—*Minding Your Ps and Qs*.

Heads Up ✦

On the keyboard, we're accustomed to using an apostrophe to indicate feet and a quotation mark to indicate inches: "The giant was 9′8″ tall." Now here's where it gets tricky. On the computer, most of us have hit the preference button so our old straight apostrophes and quotation marks are automatically replaced with *smart quotes* (' " "). In layman's terms, they're known as *curly quotes*. The problem is that curly apostrophes and quotation marks aren't the abbreviation for feet and inches. So for feet and inches, make certain your marks are straight, or what you write will be utter nonsense.

The Quotation Mark (")

Quotation marks are actually two apostrophes next to each other—double the fun with half the chance for error. Quotation marks are used when you're quoting from another work, indicating that someone is speaking, setting aside a word or phrase to show its special use, or indicating titles of works shorter than books (e.g., articles, television episodes, etc.). Let's look at each application with the rule and the dreaded *however*.

* When you are quoting from another source, enclose the passage in quotation marks.

> As K.D. Sullivan says on her website, "Make sure your message is clear, correct, and consistent."

However, if you are quoting more than just a line, the open quotation mark goes at the beginning of each new paragraph, but at the end of only the final word in the material you've quoted.

* When you want to show that someone is speaking, use quotation marks.

> Barbie said, "Ken, you drive me crazy with all your talk of gambling."

However, if you have a quote within a quote, you must use apostrophes (i.e., single quotes) within the quotation marks.

> Barbie said, "Ken explained the depth of his obsession when he told me, 'I know you hate poker, but I don't think the day is complete without sitting in on a game.'"

* Quotation marks show that you are using a word or words in a special context, such as an ironic or unusual use of a common word or when you're repeating a nickname.

> To be one of Barbie's "pets," she has to approve of how you live your life.

> When Barbie called Ken "Stud," she was referring to his hobby, poker, not his masculinity.

Heads Up ✳

Here's another place in which we have declared our independence from our British friends—the placement of punctuation around quotation marks. In England, periods and commas go outside the quotation marks. On this side of the pond, we like to confuse the issue a little. Here are the American rules:

✳ Periods and commas are *always inside* the quotation marks, even when the marks are around a title or nickname.

> Ken's latest article for *Poker Monthly* is titled "Betting on Barbie."

✳ Colons and semicolons are *always outside* the quotation marks.

> Here is the poker hand you want "according to Hoyle": a royal flush.

There are no exceptions to the outside the quotation marks rule—unless, of course, they come within the quoted material or title.

> Barbie wrote her own article, "Ante Up: What to Do When Your Pal Plays Poker."

✳ Dashes, question marks, and exclamation points are *inside* when they refer to the quoted material but *outside* when they refer to the rest of the sentence.

> Ken asked, "Are you sure that's the card you want to play?"

> How could Barbie answer anything but "I don't know"?

> Three primary rules and you're home free. Doesn't get better than that.

✳ The fourth use of quotation marks is to indicate titles of short works, magazine articles, poetry, songs, television and radio episodes, short stories, and essays. Books, plays, and television or radio series should be italicized or underlined.

"The Little Match Girl" is one of the best-known stories from *Andersen's Fairy Tales.*

Henny Penny's favorite *Sesame Street* episode was "Elmo's Chicken Dream."

The Exclamation Point (!)

Oh, my goodness! We see these everywhere! And sometimes, thanks in part to Internet chat rooms, where eager contributors make their point with an economy of words and a superfluity of symbols, we see them marching down the line like soldiers on drill. You wouldn't believe it unless you saw it with your own eyes!!!

Exclamation points most correctly follow interjections—Wow! Beautiful! Amazing! Remember in Chapter 2 we warned about using too many interjections. The occasional exclamation point spotlights your emotion. A raft of them turns the exciting dull. Be circumspect. You can get your point across with a few well-chosen phrases that convey more excitement than all the exclamation points in the world. Honest!

The Question Mark (?)

The question mark shows you're asking a question and usually ends sentences that begin with *who, what, why, when, where,* or *how*. However, you only use question marks when asking a direct question (How did Alice fall down a tiny rabbit hole?) and not an indirect question (I've often wondered how Alice fell down a tiny rabbit hole.).

There's one other use of the question mark, and it's so common that we tend to take it for granted. Enclosed in parentheses, the question mark shows the author's uncertainty about a fact or statement.

> *Alice's Adventures in Wonderland*, written in 1865(?), has become a timeless classic.

In other words, it might have been 1865 or it might have been some other year. You haven't tracked down the exact date.

The Hyphen (-)

Computers and their predecessors, word processors, have both simplified and complicated some of the punctuation marks. Once upon a typewriter, the hyphen served as both a word connector and a thought interrupter. Now, we have easily typed dashes of varying lengths, so the hyphen can go back to what it's best at—connecting words so that either the idea is unified or the meaning is made crystal clear.

Use a hyphen when you're connecting two or more words to serve as a single adjective for a noun.

The **know-it-all** Wizard of Oz didn't fool **Toto-toting** Dorothy.

Use a hyphen when you're creating a new word out of two old words. What typically happens is two words become a hyphenated word and then drift into the vocabulary as a single word. For instance, *sales person* became *sales-person*, and today it should be written without the hyphen, *salesperson*. If you're in doubt about the status of a hyphenated word, check a current dictionary. It's still the best resource around—as long as you remember to buy an updated version every few years.

Use a hyphen with the prefixes *ex-* (as in former), *self-*, and *all-* and the suffix *-elect*.

The **ex-governor**, a **self-made** man and former **all-American**, was now the **president-elect**.

Use a hyphen when writing out compound numbers or fractions.

Seventy-five animals, representing **three-quarters** of Bambi's friends, showed up to help him thrive.

Technically, if you use the fraction as the subject, you would not hyphenate it. Ergo, no hyphen is required in the following:

Three quarters of Bambi's friends showed up.

But just between us, no one pays much attention to that rule, so don't sweat it.

The Dash (—); Also Called the Em Dash

Back in the times B.C. (Before Computers), we would indicate a break in thought with two hyphens (--) and we often still do when preparing manuscripts for typesetting. But when working on a keyboard today, we can add the long dash with ease. Word processing programs make it easy to hit two keys and get the —, which is a true em dash, to emphasize and separate thoughts. You can also set your preferences so -- automatically turns into —.

Note: you'll hear about *en dashes*, too. They're the width of the letter *n*. Technically, they're used instead of the word *to* in ranges of dates, page numbers, etc., such as *1995–2005*, *pp. 50–55*, and *verses 10–12*. In truth, if you used a hyphen instead, no one would call you on it (sssh)—except editors and proofreaders like K.D., who shivered at this last statement.

Basically, the dash signifies a dramatic break in your thought.

Flopsy and Mopsy—**they hated those names**—
looked up to their brother Peter Cottontail.

Traditionally, there shouldn't be a space on either side of the em dash, but that rule is becoming looser and we see it with spaces all the time. Again, the Internet has had a profound influence. When your eyes see a sea of print on the screen, they welcome a little white space, so it's more common—and merciful—to provide it. (We talk about the differences in writing for the Internet in Chapter 9.)

Parentheses ( )

Parentheses are used in two ways: (1) to enclose figures when numbering (as we're doing right here) and (2) to set off supplemental or explanatory material, as we just did in explaining the first way. The numbering usage is self-explanatory. A parenthetical comment is very much like one set off by dashes, but without the drama. Use parentheses when you need to add information to clarify your point.

> Cinderella's coach **(a pumpkin in its first incarnation)** glittered in the moonlight.

The one thing that can trip you up with parentheses is remembering that the punctuation goes outside the parentheses, unless the parenthetical material is a complete sentence.

> Cinderella's coach glittered in the moonlight **(which was brighter than usual)**.

However,

> Cinderella's coach glittered in the moonlight. **(You'd never guess it was once a pumpkin.)**

Brackets [ ]

Brackets are used to indicate that editorial comments, corrections, or clarifications have been made.

The note said, "Sinderella [sic] has it [the glass shoe]."

[Sic] indicates that the error was in the original and isn't the fault of the writer. In the second example, *[the glass shoe]* explains what *it* refers to.

Brackets are also used when there is a parenthetical phrase within a parenthetical phrase. That's a mouthful.

Al Pacino was nominated in two categories the same year (Best Actor [*Scent of a Woman*] and Best Supporting Actor [*Glengarry Glen Ross*] in 1992) and won for Best Actor.

Brackets aren't something you'll use a lot, but you should recognize what they're telling you when you do see them.

Fifteen Punctuation Facts You Need to Know 🍁

Who knew there was so much to learn about punctuation marks? To make it as easy as possible, review the following fifteen rules from time to time and you'll be a punctuation pro:

1. A period shows where sentences end, separates the initials of some acronyms, and ends many abbreviations.
2. Don't double-space after a period at the end of a sentence; the word processing program will adjust the space for you.

3. Commas, signaling natural pauses and adding clarity to what you're writing, should be used before conjunctions and before the final *or* or *and* in a series.

4. Semicolons (weak periods) separate two thoughts of equal rank; these are thoughts that could be turned into independent sentences.

5. Colons are used to do the following: introduce lists, separate thoughts (when one further explains the other), distinguish hour and minutes, cite chapter and verse, separate the title and subtitle, and end formal salutations.

6. Ellipses indicate that words or sentences have been omitted.

7. Apostrophes show possession, not plurals (except for *its* [possession] and *it's* [it is]), as well as indicating missing letters when a verb has been contracted.

8. Quotation marks indicate that someone is speaking or that material has been taken from another source.

9. In American English, commas and periods are usually inside the quotation marks; colons and semicolons are outside; and dashes, question marks, and exclamation points are inside or outside depending on usage.

10. Exclamation points follow interjections, and you should use them very sparingly. Please!

11. Question marks show that an answer is requested or that the writer is unsure of a specific fact.

12. Hyphens connect words with prefixes, suffixes, or other words.

13. Dashes, which are about the length of the letter *m*, signify a dramatic break in thought, while shorter dashes, known

as en dashes, which are the length of the letter *n*, are used between a range of dates, times, or numbers.

14. Parentheses enclose figures in a numbered list within a sentence or set off explanatory material (facts that add substance).

15. Brackets indicate editorial comments, corrections, or clarifications or further set off text within a parenthetical phrase.

4

PRONOUNS

We Owe Them an Apology

RESPECTED LANGUAGE MAVEN William Safire claims, "When enough of us are wrong, we're right." Nice concept, but it's not going to work as a universal panacea, especially in the case of pronouns. Granted, the English language is changing, evolving kaleidoscopically, but we have to retain a basic structure around which the new usages evolve. And as much as we may want to believe that saying "him and I" is correct because everybody says it, the fact is it's wrong, it's annoying, it sounds terrible, and it's never going to fly.

In this chapter we introduce you to all the pronouns. We identify the pesky pronouns we have to deal with every day so you can see which is which and which does what to whom.

These are common words we use all the time. There aren't any hidden traps. It's simply common sense once you get the hang of it. We'll start with the basic definition: a pronoun is a word that replaces a noun.

If only it were that simple. Granted, we're not sticklers about being able to recite formal grammar rules and regulations, but there are a few dos and don'ts we have to point out. Once you get the sound of the proper pronoun in your ear, you can forget the rule. You'll know when a pronoun doesn't sound correct, and you'll wince like we do.

Basically, pronouns come in eight varieties: demonstrative, indefinite, interrogative, negative, personal, possessive, reflexive, and relative. They are much easier than that list would make them sound, so let's break the list apart and look at them one pronoun type at a time.

Demonstrative Pronouns: Dees, Dem, and Dohs

Quite simply, demonstrative pronouns show you the number and location of the noun they're replacing.

This = one thing close by. **That** = one thing at a distance.

You carry **this** chair, and I'll carry **that** lamp.

These = several things close by. **Those** = several things at a distance.

These chocolate chip cookies go in my lunch box, and **those** celery sticks remain in the refrigerator.

You can't get into too much trouble with demonstrative pronouns. Short of the "dees, dem, and dohs" types in bad gangster movies, most of us have a handle on them. They're probably the least misused of all the various words we use to replace nouns.

Indefinite Pronouns: How Many Did You Say?

Not a lot needs to be said about the indefinite pronouns except that you should know they exist because you use them—or hear them—every day. These are the vague references to uncounted numbers of people or things: *anyone, anybody, nobody, somebody, someone, everybody, everyone*, etc. Children and politicians especially like them.

But Mom, **everybody** is going except me!

Nobody else's parents make them do chores.

After school we're going over to **someone's** house to study.

Everyone in my district wants the airport extension bill passed.

Anybody will tell you I have a clear mandate.

They're easy to figure out so you won't hear them misused very often, at least not grammatically misused. Beyond that it's listener beware!

Interrogative Pronouns: Say What?

We don't always think of the question starters *who* and *what* as pronouns, but of course they are as they act as a substitute for a noun. The other interrogative pronouns are *whom*, *which*, *whose*, *whoever*, and *whatever*.

Who is going to call for pizza?

What is the number for the restaurant?

The only sticky point here is that in questions, *who* is normally going to be in the subjunctive mood. The subjunctive refers to something that could be, might be, or even should be but isn't. (*Whatever* and *whoever* also classify in this category, but their usage is more colloquial and certainly either one can be replaced by the short form.)

Heads Up *

Like *it's* and *its*, *who's* and *whose* are often confused. Just remember the two word sets work the same way.

* *Who's* is a contraction of *who is* or *who has*.
* *Whose* shows ownership.

In Chapter 5 we introduce you to the subjunctive mood. Here's the short version: when you say *if* or *wish*, use *were* instead of *was*. All together now: "the subjunctive refers to something that could be, might be, or even should be but isn't."

Oops! ✹

From the movie *Kill Bill Vol. 1*:

▌ **"Whom in Okinawa** made that steel?"

A subtitle in the duel scene between Uma Thurman and Lucy Liu toward the end of *Kill Bill Vol. 1* makes us wonder about the discussion that went on at the studio about whether it should be *who* or *whom*. Sorry, guys, you had a 50-50 chance of being right and you missed it. If the sentence had been changed to read, "That steel was made by whom in Okinawa?" then *whom* would have been correct. Of course, that's a more awkward construction, and no one would want to read all that text at the bottom of a fight scene, but they would have been vindicated grammatically.

Here's how it works. When used as an interrogative, the questioning pronoun *who* will be the subject, which means it's doing the action. Don't get tricked into saying, "Whom is at the door?" Keep in mind the title of the movie *Guess Who's Coming to Dinner?* and you'll hit the nail on the head every time. (Of course, you may run into some archaic usage like, "We are waiting for whom?"—most likely accompanied by an audible sniff—in which case the questioning pronoun becomes the object of the preposition and you want to use *whom*. Also, you are most likely speaking to a grandmother who'll never see ninety again!)

We'll delve deeply into the *who/whom* issue a little later in this chapter, but for now here's a general rule to follow: when asking questions, keep the construction simple and use *who*. You'll be right 99.9 percent of the time!

Negative Pronouns: They're Not That Difficult

A negative pronoun doesn't mean you don't like the person or thing the pronoun refers to. The negative pronouns are *none* (or *no one*), *nobody*, *nothing*, and *neither*.

The most common slipup with negative pronouns is forgetting that they take a singular verb, especially when using *none*. *None* is a contraction of *no one*, and that means it's singular. *None are* is a no-no!

> We have 270 channels available, and **none *is*** worth watching.

> **None of the teenage girls *wants*** to be seen with her mother.

> I've watched all the reality shows, and **none *relates*** to my real world.

Some of these may look and sound strange to you because most of the time we hear *none* used with a plural verb. However, if you simply replace *none* with *no one*—or if you're still not certain, with *no one of them*—you'll get it correct every time. For instance, take the first sentence. It certainly looks wrong, but see what happens when we spell out the words and make the verb plural:

> We have 270 channels available, and **no one of them *are*** worth watching.

Tell us you wouldn't say that. Please.

However, it's only fair to acknowledge that the tide is turning toward common usage rather than grammatical correctness. Some authoritative sources have already thrown in the towel and said *none are* is acceptable. We know language changes but it seems too bad that some of those changes fly in the face of good grammar and common sense.

The only other shark in the shoals to remember is that if you use *neither*, you have to use *nor*. Remember your grade school English teacher sing-songing, *"Either-or, neither-nor"*?

> **Neither** cable **nor** a satellite dish was available until I got there.

We wish every rule were that simple. Fact of the matter is a lot of us have dropped the construction altogether. Also correct:

> **Both** cable **and** a satellite dish were unavailable until I got there.

Equally correct but not as precise:

> Among the stars trying out to host the Academy Awards, **neither** Shrek **nor** Donkey had the right moves.

That's so much better than saying, "Among the stars trying out to host the Academy Awards, **only** Shrek **and** Donkey didn't have the right moves." Using *neither-nor* separates them from the rest of the pack and implies that everyone else did have the proper skills. Spoken correctly, English can be a subtly precise language.

Personal Pronouns: Be Aware, Be Very Aware

James J. Kilpatrick, whose newspaper column "The Writer's Art" has been read for decades, said, "No grammatical error is more common in English composition than the confusion of nominative pronouns (*he*, *she*, *we*, *they*) and objective pronouns (*him*, *her*, *us*, *them*). Boo-boos happen all the time, often in the most respectable surroundings." We certainly agree with him. In a half hour on the *Today* show one recent morning, Toni heard incorrect personal pronouns used three times by three different members of the cast. Before long, the incorrect begins to sound correct, especially from people we would expect to be well-versed in the language. Ouch!

Oops! 🐛

If you're making any of the following mistakes, you're in the majority—unfortunately.

From a CEO:

▌ ". . . send it directly to **he** and **me** to save time."

▌ *Should be:* ". . . send it directly to **him** and **me** to save time."

From Liz Smith's column (*New York Post*):

▌ "It was time for **Christine** and **I** to have a little talk. . . ."

Should be: "It was time for **Christine** and **me** to have a little talk. . . ."

From the *Independent*, a British newspaper:

"... some analysts had seen him as a natural successor to Dame Marjorie, **who is two years older than him.**"

Should be: "... some analysts had seen him as a natural successor to Dame Marjorie, **who is two years older than he.**"

From a William Morrow press release, reported in *Publishers Weekly*, quoting Los Angeles Deputy District Attorney Tracey Brown on her biography of her father:

"... how he raised [brother] **Michael** and I to believe anything was attainable."

Should be: "... how he raised [brother] **Michael** and **me** to believe anything was attainable."

Perhaps the most painful and plentiful mistakes we read and hear in English today involve personal pronouns—*he* versus *him*, *I* versus *me*, and *she* versus *her*. The problem seems worst when that sneaky word *and* creeps in and muddies up the water.

Looking at the examples above, no one would say, "Send it directly to he" or "It was time for I to have a little talk." Here's the trick. Erase the *and*, along with the noun or pronoun that precedes it. See? It all becomes clear. So why don't more of us know that? (It's especially disturbing that the last example slipped through a publishing house, a publishing magazine, and a well-educated attorney. Any wonder the rest of us make mistakes?)

In situations like *older than him*, mentally add the word *is* after the pronoun (*him* in this example). No one would be tempted to say

> . . . Dame Marjorie, who is two years older than **him** is.

> *Should be:* . . . Dame Marjorie, who is two years older than **he** is.

The simple act of stretching out the sentence will almost always give you the correct pronoun to use.

Let's see if we can make it easier for you to choose the perilous personal pronouns correctly.

In Chapter 2 we talked about subjects and objects. These are two of the root grammar principles you have to learn in any language, and they're especially important when you encounter a personal pronoun.

Heads Up ✹

The subject is *doing* the action.
The object is *receiving* the action.

The pronoun you choose—*I* or *me*, *he* or *him*, *she* or *her*, *we* or *us*, *they* or *them*—will depend on whether you're referring to a subject that's doing the action or an object that's receiving it.

Under the balcony, **Romeo** (subject) patiently awaited **Juliet** (object).

He (subject) patiently awaited **her** (object).

She (subject) kept **him** (object) waiting on purpose.

When the pronoun follows a preposition (*in, or, if, between, by, for,* etc.), it always becomes the object of the preposition.

The balcony wouldn't hold both **Romeo** and **Juliet**.

The balcony wouldn't hold both **him** and **her**.

To choose the correct personal pronoun, all you have to do is decide whether you need a subject or an object and then choose the one that fits.

Heads Up

Subject Pronouns	Object Pronouns
I, we	me, us
you	you
he, she, it, they	him, her, it, them

Deciding whether to choose a subject or object pronoun is also important if the construction gets a little more complicated.

The old family feud infuriated **Harriet Hatfield** and **Mickey McCoy**.

Would you ever say the following?

The old family feud infuriated **she** and **he**.

Didn't think so.

We've purposely left out a personal pronoun—*one*—as in, "One wonders when Madam will be home for tea." While still heard across the Atlantic, that construction is as outdated stateside as butlers and coming home for tea.

Reporters and columnists used to regularly say *one* in an attempt to remove themselves from the event they were describing or the opinions they were sharing. The trend today is toward informality. This is thanks in large part to the more casual language of the Internet and the popularity of the online journals (blogs) in which writers "let it all hang out." So now you'll hear reporters say, "We heard the explosion in Baghdad," instead of, "One felt a sense of history at the Yalta Conference."

Instead of *one*, use *I*, as in, "I wonder when Madam will be home for tea."

Heads Up

Here are a couple of usages of pronouns that might trip you up.

Ships, countries, swords, airplanes, and storms have traditionally been referred to as *she* instead of *it*. This usage is beginning to change, but don't be surprised if you hear

She's a beautiful ship, and I've enjoyed every minute I sailed on **her**.

Nouns like company, army, business, etc., are referred to as *it*. If you're talking about a company, refer to it as *that*, not *who*.

▌A company **that** has a social conscience is a special organization indeed.

Possessive Pronouns: You Can Own Them!

Like our friends the demonstrative pronouns, possessive pronouns are pretty clear-cut. Anything we refer to as belonging to ourselves or to someone else is going to be *mine, your, yours, his, her, hers, its, our, ours, their,* or *theirs.*

> **Our** birthday party also celebrated **their** anniversary, **his** promotion, and a host of other unrelated occasions.

The only fly in the ointment is to make sure you use a plural pronoun when you replace a plural noun.

> **The DeVille babies** were twins, and both **Phil** and **Lil** were Rugrats.

> **They** were twins, and both **he** and **she** were Rugrats.

Ah, yes, you say, that's fine—but what about *its?* What about it indeed! We talk again about *its* in Chapter 6 because it seems to be so universally misused.

Heads Up ☀

In a nutshell, here's what you have to remember about *its* vs. *it's*:

☀ *Its* means *it* has a possession.
☀ *It's* means *it is*—*it* has an action.

So if you're using *it's* as a possessive pronoun, save your-self an apostrophe.

Quantifiers: How Many, How Much

Quantifiers aren't usually considered one of the pronoun varieties, but these words are used with both nouns and pronouns to tell us how much of something we're talking about. The most common quantifiers are words like *some, much, many, few, little, a lot, several, most, half, three*, etc. They can be a single word or a phrase.

Why are they important when talking about pronouns? Simply because most quantifiers are separated from the pronoun by a preposition, usually *of* or sometimes *to*. This tells us that the pronoun has to be in the objective case, not the subjective.

> **Some** of **them** looked pretty tasty, but **a few** of **them** were spoiled.

> The public praise and private adoration meant **a lot** to **her**.

> Give **half** of the sandwich to **me** and **the rest** to **him**.

Notice that it's almost impossible to use quantifiers without a preposition. Remember to be objective about quantifiers, and they won't be a problem.

Reflexive Pronouns: Right Back at You!

When we were talking to friends and business acquaintances about this book, one of the most often heard comments was, "Don't forget about *myself*!" That was good news because it meant we weren't the only ones who dislike it when *myself* is thrown into sentences indiscriminately, like extra salt in the stew.

The *self* pronouns—*myself, yourself, himself, herself, itself, ourselves, yourselves,* and *themselves*—are only used in two distinct applications:

* When you want to toss the focus back to the subject
* When you want to draw extra attention or emphasis to the person

When you want to toss the focus back to the subject:

Even taking precautions, I cut **myself** with the knife.

Quaking with fear, he let **himself** into the old ghost house.

We watched **ourselves** on the quiz show and laughed **ourselves** silly.

For us, this is the primary time the *self* pronouns make sense. No one would say any of the following:

I cut **me** with the knife.

He let **him** into the house.

We watched **us** . . . and laughed **us** silly.

They grate on the ear—and don't always convey the situation accurately. For times like these, the *self* pronouns are a necessary and valid construction.

When you want to draw extra attention or emphasis to the person (that means you want another way to stress the person you're talking about):

Mother, I'd rather do it **myself**!

The contest winner **himself** admitted he was given the answers.

They **themselves** offered to pay back the money, thus sparing their kneecaps.

While the *self* pronouns are used in these examples for emphasis or focus, notice that they could be omitted and the sentences would still make sense. Their only purpose is to add a verbal underlining to the thought being communicated. They become a visual stressor. For instance, read those same sentences putting the emphasis on the first noun or pronoun, and you'll have the identical meaning without using *self*.

Mother, **I'd** rather do it!

The contest winner admitted he was given the answers.

They offered to pay back the money, thus sparing their kneecaps.

What we hear too often is *myself* being used in place of *I* or *me*, as in the following examples:

Myself and three friends are going to play paintball in the forest preserve.

The Chartreuse Team included John, Henry, Samantha, and **myself**.

Not sure if it's right? Take out that pesky *and*, along with the nouns directly before or after it, in the first examples.

Myself is going to play paintball in the forest preserve.

The Chartreuse Team included **myself**.

Nope. It won't fly. Obviously you want to say

I am going to play paintball in the forest preserve.

The Chartreuse Team included **me**.

Use *I* and *me* instead.

Sometimes we get the feeling people use *myself* because it makes them feel they've somehow added a note of refinement to their language. Using the *self* pronouns incorrectly actually gives the opposite impression. Think Archie Bunker talking about "myself and the Dingbat." You certainly never hear the oh-so-sophisticated Miss Piggy slip up and say, "It's *moi-même*."

So when *do* you use the *self* pronouns? Except for the first application—tossing the focus back to the subject—you're probably safer to just avoid them.

Relative Pronouns: Whom Cares?

Whom cares which pronoun we use? Very few, it would seem.

For a time during the last decades of the twentieth century, *whom* virtually disappeared from all but the most formal writing. Even the professional grammar mavens advocated dropping *whom* altogether. The advent of a more casual culture had caused the *who/whom* debate to become much too much trouble to worry about. Instead, *who* was used almost universally, and it didn't seem to herald the end of civilization as we know it.

Somehow, the new millennium brought with it a new awareness of the power of language, and *whom* made a reentry into the vocabulary—with a vengeance. Instead of being ignored, *whom* today seems to be used indiscriminately. In this case, more is definitely less.

Oops!

From *The New York Times* on the movie *Kinsey*:

▌ "In Mr. Condon's version, Wardell Pomeroy, a research assistant played by Chris O'Donnell, walks out in disgust, leaving Kinsey alone to face **the monster whom** his refusal to moralize about sex seems to have conjured up."

Granted, there are a number of things editors could argue with in that sentence, but the use of *whom* is particularly strange and jarring.

The easiest way to remember which to use is that *who* is a subject, and so it performs some sort of action. *Whom* is an object, and that means it is being done to, not doing.

Heads Up 🔥

Remember that *who* will always do something to *whom*.

At this point it would be easy but nonproductive to give lots of complicated examples of when *whom* is appropriate even though it doesn't seem to be. That's not the point of this exercise. Because we do so much writing and editing in the areas of business, consumer publications, audio scripts, and the Internet, we're firm believers in keeping the language simple. If the sentence that's puzzling you is so convoluted that you can't figure out the subject and object, then we'd respectfully suggest you rewrite it into a more streamlined thought or, at the very least, break it up into more than one sentence. That will almost always clear up any confusion.

Another pair of relative pronouns that give people fits and starts is *that/which*. Here again we have decided to discuss them in greater detail in Chapter 6 because they are among the most often misused of all the pronouns.

Heads Up 🔥

Here's the short drill: in most cases, use *that* and you'll probably be correct. When a part of the sentence is set off in commas and can be dropped without losing the sense of what you're saying, use *which*.

▌ The short stories **that** O. Henry wrote are still a delight.

▌ The story **that** is my favorite was made into a movie, **which** was too bad.

One point we do have to make concerns the less often used relative pronouns *whosoever* and *whomsoever*. Most of the time when we hear these words we think of the Bible.

> That **whosoever** should believe in him should not perish but have eternal life. (John 3:15)

> The Most High ruleth in the kingdom of men and giveth it to **whomsoever** he will. (Daniel 4:17)

Look up *whomsoever* on Internet search engines, and you'll find several hits for general notices addressed *To Whomsoever It May Concern*. Save yourself the extra letters. In almost any situation, *who*, *whom*, and *what* will work just fine and sound much more contemporary than *whomsoever*.

In short, our advice on the relative pronouns echoes the advice we always give: when in doubt, keep it simple and you'll be a winner.

Heads Up ✹

Whatsoever sounds as if it should be included with these pronouns, but it is an adjective and modifies a noun instead of replacing it. *Whatsoever* refers to an unspecified amount.

▌ No money **whatsoever** is left in the account, even though I still have checks.

▌ Give him **whatsoever** ingredients are in the fridge and the chef will create a gourmet meal.

Twelve Pronoun Facts You Need to Know ✹

With these twelve pronoun facts, you can be confident you won't make a mistake again:

1. A pronoun is a word that replaces a noun.
2. When asking questions about an unknown person, keep the construction simple and use *who,* not *whom.*
3. Negative pronouns take a singular verb.
4. Pronoun errors can often be caught by removing the nouns directly before or after the *and* in the sentence.
5. Pronouns are either subjects or objects.
6. When a pronoun follows a preposition, the pronoun is in the objective case.
7. Pronouns need to have the verb agree.
8. *Its* means *it* has a possession. (*It's* means *it is*—*it* has an action.)

9. Quantifiers tell *how much* and take the object pronoun.
10. The *self* pronouns are for focus or emphasis, but they can often be avoided altogether.
11. *Who* will always do something to *whom*.
12. *That* refers to essential action; *which* follows a comma and typically precedes nonessential information.

Tackling Verbs with Verve

Where would we be without verbs? Dullsville, that's where. Nothing would ever happen. Think of a world with only nouns and pronouns and adjectives sitting around trying to figure out what to do with themselves. Verbs allow us to escalate and renovate and perambulate and cerebrate, to travel and unravel, to ramble and scramble and fumble and tumble. They are the words that put life in our nouns and propel us into action.

Verbs put the pizzazz in what we're saying. They make a movie out of a still picture. They convey what the subject (noun or pronoun) is going to do or has done, and they explain what's happening to the object (another noun or pronoun). They come in different shapes and sizes. They can move you or leave you yawning. In this chapter we're going to examine the pesky but essential action words that we use and abuse every day.

Transitive vs. Intransitive Verbs

We covered some of the wonders of verbs in Chapter 2, but we didn't talk about how they are either transitive or intransitive—or both. You really don't have to remember the names. What you have to know is that some verbs take an object (*transitive*) and some don't (*intransitive*)—and some can go either way.

A transitive verb has to have an object to complete its meaning.

> The reviewer's praise **put** (verb) *stars* (object) in the ingénue's eyes.

> The comedian **laid** (verb) *an egg* (object) before he got to his second joke.

An intransitive verb doesn't have an object. These are verbs like *go*, *sit*, or *be*.

> Ramona **sat** quietly waiting for the tooth fairy to visit her brother.

> To stay serene, **go** with the flow.

> "I **think**, therefore I **am**."

Now comes the fun part. There are verbs that can be transitive or intransitive, depending on how you use them.

The tenor sang (intransitive) well, but **he didn't sing** (transitive) the song we requested.

Knowing these differences may not be essential to speaking English correctly, but there is a benefit. When your youngster asks you if you know the difference between transitive and intransitive verbs, you'll be on top of it. That's how we learned!

To complete this lesson, you should know that transitive verbs can usually be changed from active to passive voice. Intransitive verbs can't. Stop frowning. We'll explain *voice* next.

Verbs Have Voices

Verbs have two voices to choose from, *active* and *passive*. If a verb is in the active voice, the subject is doing the action.

The matador **confronted** the bull, **stared** him in the eye, **flicked** his cape, then **ran** back to the side of the arena.

The passive verb always uses some tense of *to be*.

The book that **was written** in four weeks **was made** into a movie in four years.

The subject of a passive verb never acts—which gets pretty boring. It's like listening to music that's always in a minor key. Dreary. So writing or talking in the active voice is best. To see why, let's take the last example and turn it around.

She wrote the book in four weeks, but **it took** four years to make the movie.

You want others to remember what you say and write, so keep it active. The exercise will do you good.

Regular Verbs

To use a verb correctly, you have to be able to conjugate it, which means give the present tense, the past tense, and the past participle. Let's look at a regular verb.

Begin with the infinitive (the verb with *to* in front); then you need to know the present and past tense form, the past participle, and the gerund.

	Present	Past	Past Participle	Gerund
to listen	listen	listened	listened	listening
to repeat	repeat	repeated	repeated	repeating
to sweep	sweep	swept	swept	sweeping

Note: regular verbs form their past tense and past participle by adding -*ed*, -*d*, or -*t* to the present tense. The gerund, which turns a verb into a noun, is formed by adding -*ing* to the present tense.

Once you know the major parts of a verb, you ought to be able to use it easily. The present tense is for an action happening right now.

I **listen** (present) to what you say.

The past tense describes an action that already occurred.

I **listened** (past) to you last week, too.

The past participle combines with an auxiliary verb to express a completed action in the past.

I **have listened** (past participle) to you for years.

The gerund is a verb functioning as a noun.

Listening (gerund) gives me a headache, even though you don't say anything.

Heads Up 🍁

The rules governing the use of gerunds are many and complicated. The best bet is to avoid them when you can.

So-called *i-n-g* words are generally considered weak additions to your language. Obviously, when you're describing a continued action in the past, you can say, "The elephant had been stomping the grapes without complaint." That's OK. But a simple "The elephant stomped the grapes without complaint" is just as correct and more to the point.

Auxiliary Verbs

There are two types of auxiliary verbs, *primary* and *modal*. (You can forget those terms, too. We're just showing off.) You need to know that *be*, *have*, and *do* are auxiliary verbs that can function as verbs on their own. That's why they're called *primary*. *Can, could, may, might, must, ought to, shall, should, will, would,* and *used to* are modal verbs and need to be combined with a second verb if they're going to mean anything. We use these auxiliary verbs to form all the other tenses of verbs. For instance, English is a language that doesn't have a verb form for the future tense. Instead, we take the present tense and add *shall* or *will* to it.

> When the circus arrives, I **shall be** in the front row to see the acrobats fall.

> After the aerialist lands in the net, he **will bound** to his feet as if he meant it to happen.

The use of *shall* seems to be declining, and the multipurpose *will* is taking its place. Here's a hint: contract the verb (e.g., *I will* to *I'll, he will* to *he'll, they will* to *they'll*) and no one will ever know which you're using.

Not All Verbs Are Regular

The first thing to learn about verbs is that when you think you've got a handle on them, you find a batch of irregular verbs that don't conjugate in the typical way.

If a verb won't play by the rules of conjugation, it's termed *irregular*—and there are hundreds of them in English. Do not despair, because most of them are so common that you use them every day. For instance, the verb *to write (write, wrote, written)* is irregular, which we've found is quite often true of a career in writing as well. The commonplace irregulars are pretty easy. The others you will just have to learn.

The most common irregular verb in almost every language is *to be*. Just as life is unpredictable, this verb takes its own path and seems to follow no rules at all: *I am*, *you are*, *he is*, *we are*, *you are*, *they are*. Then in the past tense, *was* and *were* come out of nowhere. We'll have a few choice words on the verb *to be* a little later on in this chapter.

Yes, Verbs Have Moods, Too

As we've said, this isn't a text on the mysteries of grammar. We're not here to talk about past pluperfect intransitive verbs. Frankly, very few people could tell you what they are, and most of us don't much care. That being said, there are a few things we do have to mention.

You should know that English verbs have moods, just like the rest of us. There are three moods. Two we use all the time.

The *indicative mood*, the most basic and often used, states a fact or asks a question.

The Cat Show is televised every year. **Did you see** the alley cat that won?

The *imperative mood* (think backseat driver) gives a command.

Slow down now! **Watch out** for the pedestrian! **Turn** left right here!

The *subjunctive mood* states a wish, expresses what might have been (but probably won't be), or indicates a command or request.

I wish I were taller so I would be thinner.

If **I were** king of the world, I would abolish the subjunctive mood.

It's essential that the king **be accorded** every courtesy.

The subjunctive mood isn't as well recognized as the indicative or imperative, so it gets mangled a good share of the time. Any verb can be used in the subjunctive mood; however, most of the mistakes are made with the verb *to be*.

Heads Up ❋

The rules are as follows:

❋ When the action expressed may never happen or is false or improbable, use *were* instead of *was*.

❋ If the action is something you would like to have happen but that probably won't, use *were* instead of *was*.

❋ If you are making a demand, use *be* instead of *am*.

Pure and simple, the words *if* and *wish*, or any command or request, take the subjunctive mood of the verb *to be* (i.e., *be* or *were*, not *am* or *was*).

Listen to the Jerry Bock and Sheldon Harnick musical *Fiddler on the Roof*, and you'll hear Tevye singing, "If I were a rich man. . . ." Notice that he doesn't say, "If I *was* a rich man. . . ." Obviously lyricist Sheldon Harnick understood that Tevye and wealth were never going to happen, so he used the subjunctive. A good test is to add the word *but* to the sentence. If it fits with the sense of the sentence, you need the subjunctive.

If I were a rich man, **(but I'll never be)**. . . .

If I were to win the lottery, I'd be happy **(but I'd have to buy a ticket first)**.

Wish is another word that often implies an action that's not going to happen and so it also takes the subjunctive.

I wish I were (not **was**) king of the world so I could change the rules.

Demands and requests also require this tense, in this case using *be* instead of *am*:

Kermit always demands that he **be** (not **is**) seated by the pool.

Miss Piggy's ego requires that she **be** (not **is**) the center of attention.

When Toni's daughter, Cait, was a toddler, she announced to her mother, "I wish it wasn't raining so we could go to the zoo." Said Toni, repeating by rote what had been drummed into her head starting at the same age, "I wish it *weren't* raining—wish takes the subjunctive." Said Cait, "I don't care! I still want to go to the zoo." That sums up how most of us feel about the subjunctive. However, we promised to give you the necessary tools to speak English correctly, and *if we were* to ignore the subjunctive, you would *insist we not be* derelict in our duty.

The Infinitive Myth

Mischief and mayhem are fine, but never split an infinitive! In the eyes of most English teachers, there are very few infractions of life's great rules that come close to the horror and shame of putting some extraneous word between *to* and *explain* (or whatever your verb of choice might be). If that's what you learned—and we sure did—now's the time to unlearn it.

Some wise old grammarians, probably *to once-and-for-all justify* a ridiculous admonition, went plodding through the thousands of volumes of English rules and regulations and found we've been conned. The rule doesn't exist. All those red marks on essay tests and high school themes were put there in error. There's absolutely no reason *to savagely defend* the sanctity of the infinitive.

That's right. It's perfectly fine *to wantonly split* the infinitive. If you want *to coldheartedly separate* the verb from its introductory word, you go right ahead. Whew! One less rule *to needlessly worry* about.

That said, sometimes there's nothing cleaner than an infinitive that doesn't suffer from adverbial desecration. Think Hamlet: "to be or not to be." "To maybe be or not to really be" doesn't have the same punch. So it's a matter of style and not grammar. Split that infinitive when you need to, and keep it pure when it strengthens the thought.

Let's Have a Little Agreement

One of the flies in the verb ointment is how the noun (or pronoun) and verb agree—or don't. We're only going to cover the situations most of us run into every day.

It's pretty much a no-brainer that if you use an obviously singular noun you match it with a singular verb, while a plural noun takes a plural verb. *I* is singular, just like *he*, *she*, and *it*. *You*, *we*, and *they* are plural.

> When **one candy bar *is*** too many, **several candy bars *are*** not enough.

Often a single subject is separated from the verb by plural words. The secret is to remove those other words and you'll quickly find out whether your subject is singular or plural.

> **Mary**, along with her lambs and the other shepherdesses, ***was*** happiest in the meadow.

In general, when subjects are joined by *and*, they take a plural verb.

> **Mutt and Jeff *make*** a strange-looking pair.

Oops! 💥

In a display ad for Chicago's National City Theater presentation of "Conway & Korman Together Again," this line appeared in boldfaced type:

▌ **"Tim and Harvey *has* formed** one of the most loved comedy teams ever."

Obviously *has formed* should be *have formed* since two of them are in on the action. A lot of people saw that ad before it was printed and didn't catch the error. However, it's only fair to note that in the next Sunday's edition of the *Chicago Tribune* the ad had been corrected.

When subjects are joined by *either-or* or *neither-nor*, they take a singular verb. If one subject is plural and the other singular, make the verb agree with the subject closest to it.

Neither Esmerelda **nor her teachers** *were* aware she was a genius.

Neither her teachers **nor Esmerelda** *was* aware she was a genius.

As we pointed out in Chapter 4 when discussing the pronouns *each*, *every*, *none*, *nobody*, *anybody*, *somebody*, all the pronouns in this category take singular verbs, despite what some dictionaries are now allowing. We continue to hold firm on *none is*, but various grammar authorities are caving in under the pressure of common misusage and allowing *none are*. Brrrr. To us, it's like nails on a blackboard.

When the subject is collective—that is, a noun that refers to several things (e.g., *family*, *army*, *number*, *school*, *coven*, *government*, etc.)—you're almost always safe using a singular verb. There is a rule that if you're talking about the individual members of the group instead of the group as a whole, you should use the plural verb, but that's not a deal-breaker. Most people who will call you on that technicality need to get a life.

The university *was* offering a Ph.D. in cheerleading despite academic concerns.

The family *has* (could be *have*) a few sharks in the gene pool.

If you want to be perfectly correct, think if you could add *individuals* or *members* or *persons* after the collective noun. Then you know if it's singular or plural. In the first example, you wouldn't say "The university individuals (or members or faculty) were offering a Ph.D. . . ." It's the university as a unit that was offering it. In the second example, it could be the entire family or family members who are in peril.

Phrasal Verbs

In English, rather than come up with a new verb for each subtle distinction, we idiomatically follow the root verb with an adverb or a preposition, called a *particle*. (You don't have to remember that. There won't be a test.) The best way to explain phrasal verbs is to take a word like *run*. In order to express the nuances of *run*, we add particles and get *run across, run away, run down, run for, run from, run in, run into, run over, run to, run through, run up*, etc.—each one of which changes the meaning of the verb. Most other languages would have a totally different word for each of those activities. You can see another side of the particle in the "What's Up?" that follows.

What's Up? 🐾

This piece has been showing up on the Internet for years without attribution. We salute whoever wrote it.

We've got a two-letter word we use constantly that may have more meaning than any other. The word is **up.**

It is easy to understand **up,** *meaning toward the sky or toward the top of a list. But when we waken, why do we wake* **up**? *At a meeting, why does a topic come* **up**, *why do participants speak* **up**, *and why are the officers* **up** *for election? And is it* **up** *to the secretary to write* **up** *a report?*

> *Often the little word isn't needed, but we use it anyway. We brighten* **up** *a room, fix* **up** *the old car, and polish* **up** *the silver. At other times, it has special meanings. People stir* **up** *trouble, work* **up** *an appetite, get tied* **up** *in traffic. To be dressed is one thing, but to be dressed* **up** *is special. It may be confusing, but a drain must be opened* **up** *because it is stopped* **up**. *We open* **up** *a store in the morning and close it* **up** *at night. We seem to be mixed* **up** *about* **up**.
>
> *To be* **up** *on the proper use of* **up**, *look* **up** *the word in your dictionary. In one desk-size dictionary,* **up** *takes* **up** *half a page, and listed definitions add* **up** *to about forty. If you are* **up** *to it, you might try building* **up** *a list of the many ways in which* **up** *is used. It will take* **up** *a lot of your time but, if you don't give* **up**, *you may wind* **up** *with a thousand.*

Here's the catch. Sometimes the verb and the preposition can be separated without damaging the sentence.

Simon **ran** the documents **through** the shredder as the FBI entered the room.

For clarity and structure, most times it's preferable to keep the phrasal verb intact to avoid getting sentences like these:

". . . a play area was going to be added for the inmates to **interact** with their children **in**." (Olivia Goldsmith, *Pen Pals*)

"Dyer, John. I'm pretty sure I didn't **dream** this British poet **up**." (A. J. Jacobs, *The Know-It-All*)

Stop! The first rule of any language is to communicate, and if we have to get out a road map to figure out what you're trying to say, someone is going to get lost. Think how much clearer each of these sentences would be if the phrasal verb had been kept intact, as follows:

> . . . a play area was going to be added for the inmates to **interact in** with their children.

> Dyer, John. I'm pretty sure I didn't **dream up** this British poet.

We could give you long lists of phrasal verbs that can and can't be separated, but it's just as easy for you to *look at* the sentence you've written and *figure out* whether you've *broken up* the verb inappropriately.

K.D.'s Proofreading Perspective ✳

Here's another verb issue that gets overlooked. In titles, *all* verbs should have the first letter capitalized—even those short words like *Is* and *Are*.

Beware the Dreaded *to Be* Verb

Let's get this out of the way because we can already hear the hue and cry that will arise from writing coaches who consider using *to be* verbs just short of passing on the plague.

We learned in school that the verb *to be*, like most of our existence, is irregular. It doesn't follow the other verb patterns. Therefore, let's take a closer look at it. In the following table, you'll find the basic conjugation of the verb. We won't even go into "woulda, shoulda, coulda been" or any of the other forms of this most essential verb. Think! Without it, we wouldn't be. We couldn't exist.

So what do our writing instructors tell us right off the bat? Do not use *to be* verbs. Period. No argument allowed. We disagree. No surprise there.

Conjugation of the Verb *to Be*

	Present	*Past*	*Future*
1st person singular (I)	am	was	will be
2nd person singular (you)	are	were	will be
3rd person singular (he, she, it)	is	was	will be
1st person plural (we)	are	were	will be
2nd person plural (you)	are	were	will be
3rd person plural (they)	are	were	will be

Past Participle: been
Gerund: being

We're going to get into trouble here with some of the stiff-in-the-bit types, but here goes. It's impossible to totally avoid *to be* verbs. They're everywhere. Some of the greatest passages in literature hang on *to be* verbs. Hamlet's "*to be* or not *to be*" soliloquy aside, Sydney Carton, the hero of Charles Dickens's *A Tale of Two Cities*, begins the book with this epic piece of parallel construction: "*It was* the best of times, *it was* the worst of times, *it was* the age of wisdom, *it was* the age of foolishness, *it was* the epoch of belief, *it was* the epoch of incredulity, *it was* the season of Light, *it was* the season of Darkness, *it was* the spring of hope, *it was* the winter of despair." There are a few *to be* verbs for you. Here are some other classic opening lines:

"**It was** a bright cold day in April, and the clocks were striking thirteen." (George Orwell, *1984*)

"**It was** love at first sight." (Joseph Heller, *Catch-22*)

"Happy families **are** all alike; every unhappy family **is** unhappy in its own way." (Leo Tolstoy, *Anna Karenina*)

"**Who is** John Galt?" (Ayn Rand, *Atlas Shrugged*)

Would the fervid writing gurus, with their hatred of *to be*, have changed those lines to utilize a more powerful verb? Perhaps as "Explain John Galt" or "Can anyone shed light on the true nature of John Galt?" We hope not.

Heads Up ✳

The fact is that the *to be* verb is perfectly fine when it's called for. It serves a great purpose. It conveys a clean, clear message without fuss or bother.

However, if you are using *to be* because you're too lazy to come up with something else, then we have to talk.

Verbs carry your thought through the sentence. The stronger you can make those verbs, the stronger your message is going to be. Sometimes, nothing is more powerful than the simple elegance of *to be*. It's often the best choice for the situation. Other times, you may want to substitute another verb or reorganize the sentence completely.

The day **was** hot, and we **were** lazy while we **were** at the pool.

Better: The hot day contributed to our laziness while we lounged poolside.

Nick and Nora **were** tired, but Asta **was** ready for a walk.

Better: Although tired, Nick and Nora walked Asta around the cemetery.

It seems that the urge to purge the *to be* verb isn't limited to writing instructors. Increasingly, we hear it left out of newscasts. Listen carefully next time the tube is on, and you'll find *to be* has, as reporters say, "gone missing." (Don't even get us started on that usage!)

The president [**was**] in Great Britain today for meetings.

A four-footed killer [**is**] stalking family pets in the hillside area, so neighbors [**are**] warned to be cautious.

What happened to verbs? They seem to have disappeared as if the newscaster were reading the crawl instead of regular copy. We would mount a campaign calling for the replacement of missing verbs, but we'd just be spinning our wheels.

Usages to Avoid

While we're firmly planted on our soapbox, we want to say a few words about commonly misused verbs. These are verbs that must be followed by an adverb or a preposition, but increasingly that second word is missing. We're not talking about the phrasal verbs that require the second word for meaning. We mean the verbs that call for a second word but no one's listening. Let's begin with Toni's top nails-on-the-blackboard mistake: *graduate school*. Here are three examples for the "Oops!" column.

Oops!

"Michael Daly is the first American-born in his family. He attended 16 grammar schools. He **graduated Yale University**." (*New York Daily News*)

"The high-tech wizardry is so state-of-the-art advanced that you have **to graduate MIT** just to turn on the bathroom lights." (*New York Post*)

"Then, in the years **since graduating college**, I began a long, slow slide into dumbness." (A. J. Jacobs, *The Know-It-All*)

Then we have a half-oops:

"We've had 20 students **graduate from college** before they were 20. We've got three 13-year-olds **graduating high school**." (memory expert Howard Berg, quoted in the *Chicago Tribune*)

Please, no more. We hear it every day. We read it constantly. It's so commonplace that it must sound correct to most people. (We especially like Howard Berg, who forgot how to use the verb correctly the second time it appeared in the paragraph.)

Ask any jeweler. You *graduate pearls* (that is, you put them in ascending or descending order by size). Ergo, unless you're sizing your learning institutions, you *graduate* **from** *school*.

However,

> My two-year-old son **graduated from** Sam's Obedience School. The school also **graduated** three terriers, two poodles, and a sheepdog.

Notice, *the school graduates you*, but *you graduate from* it. *Babysit* is another verb that makes us wince.

> I have **to babysit** [for] my brother, so I can't meet the guys for hoops tonight.

> **Babysitting** [for] Eloise means a day at the Plaza.

Just as you graduate from a school, you *babysit for* a child—or as the purists might point out, you babysit for the parents, as they're the ones with the cash. In fairness, we should point out that the use of *for* with *babysit* is beginning to go the way of other niceties. We can only imagine what a book like this will be endorsing as correct usage in 2050.

If we keep dropping the prepositions from verbs that need them, before long we're going to be speaking in shorthand. Words don't cost you anything. You can add another without running up a bill.

Ten Rules to Tackle All Those Verbs with Verve ✳

We've given you a lot of information on verbs. Here's what you really have to remember:

1. Verbs make your words dance and sing and move about.
2. Some verbs take an object (transitive) and some don't (intransitive)—and some can go either way.

3. Verbs have two voices: active, in which the subject does the action, and passive, in which the action is done by the direct object.
4. Verbs are either regular, which are easy, or irregular, which you have to learn individually.
5. Verbs come in three moods: indicative, imperative, and subjunctive.
6. It's perfectly OK to wantonly split an infinitive.
7. Verbs have to agree with the subject of the sentence, which can be singular, plural, or collective.
8. Some English verbs change their meaning when a particle is added to the root verb—e.g., *go around, go back, go into, go over, go through*, etc.
9. Used correctly, *to be* verbs are perfectly acceptable, but when the situation calls for a memorable verb, choose something else.
10. Some verbs take adverbs or prepositions to make sense—e.g., *graduate from* and *babysit for*.

6

It's Only a Word — What Does It Matter?

HAVE YOU EVER struggled to find just the right word only to come up with one that was close, but no cigar? In this chapter we talk about words—which ones to use and why to use them. We discuss word sets that seem to most often give our clients fits and starts.

In the earlier chapters, you had some large—and we hope not too painful—lessons in the basics of English, including the oh-so-sinned-against pronouns. You should now understand why picking the correct pronoun is vital if you're going to hold the respect of your audience whether you're speaking or writing. The same is true of picking the correct word when faced with a potentially confusing choice. The right word can seal the deal, and the wrong word can brand you as, at best, inattentive and, at worst, illiterate.

In this chapter we're going to talk about words that are commonly misused and how you can clean up your act if you're sometimes befuddled by what word to put in which sentence and why.

Fifty Sets of Commonly Confused Words

The following fifty sets of words perplex nearly everyone from time to time. This list will help you keep them straight and use them correctly. As is our wont, we'll not only define them for you and give you the part of speech, but we'll also give examples so you can keep them straight. Along the way, you'll also find a few editorial comments, where we voice our frustrations, which probably mirror some of yours, or try to clear murky waters.

In the interest of clarity, we use the following abbreviations for the parts of speech:

(n) noun
(pr) pronoun
(adj) adjective
(v) verb
(adv) adverb
(prep) preposition
(conj) conjunction

1. accept   to receive willingly (v)
   except   to exclude (v)

   Except for the tarantula, her parents cheerfully **accepted** all of Hermione's new pets.

2. advice   suggestion or counsel (n)
   advise   to give advice (v)

I **advise** you to take with a grain of salt your mother's **advice** that you become a chef.

3. affect   to influence (v)
   effect   result (n)

The stone-faced psychiatrist wondered whether she had witnessed the desired **effect** when she tried to **affect** a patient's behavior.

We can't just leave it there. *Effect* is a versatile word that can be combined with either *in* or *to the* or *into*, any one of which changes its meaning.

In effect means "virtually" or "in substance."

In exchange for earlier parole, the prisoners agreed to what was **in effect** a reduction of their liberties.

To the effect means "saying without actually spelling it out."

The warden, sensing a revolt, issued a statement **to the effect** that he would resign if the situation demanded.

Into effect means that something has become operative—in other words, that it is now functioning.

The new parole plan was put **into effect** immediately.

The rule to remember is that when you're using a *noun*, you'll most often want to use *effect*. When you're using a *verb*, you'll almost always use *affect*.

4. aggravate   to make a situation worse (v)
   irritate   to annoy or be annoyed by someone or something (v)

The mime was **irritated** when the expensive medicine only **aggravated** his twitching.

5. all ready   the state of being prepared (adv)
   already   concerning something that happened previously (adv)

The boys were **all ready** to chow down at the sports award banquet, although they had **already** eaten twice that afternoon.

6. allot   to assign a portion or distribute by lottery (v)
   a lot   a great deal, frequently (n)

A lot of the playoff tickets were **allotted** on a first-come, first-served basis.

7. anxious   uneasy (adj)
   eager   enthusiastic (adj)

The bride was **eager** to be married but **anxious** about her new in-laws.

K.D.'s Proofreading Perspective ✹

Yay! This is one of my favorites. I'm correcting people on *eager* and *anxious* all the time, and I'm glad to see that though a lot of words with similar connotations are being used interchangeably, the dictionary still supports me, and there really is a difference between what these two words mean. And by the way, now that you are reading this book and will know so many cool new rules, let me give you a caution. Not everyone will appreciate your correcting them—no matter how well meaning your intentions or how awful their error. Just give them a knowing smile and let it go.

8. appraise   to place a value on something (v)
   apprise   to inform (v)

After **appraising** the ancient clock, the *Antiques Roadshow* expert **apprised** both the owner and the audience of its value.

9. biweekly   every two weeks (adj)
   semiweekly   twice a week (adj)

Pets and Pests magazine was so popular it went from **biweekly** (26 issues) to **semiweekly** (104 issues) after just one year.

Just to confuse the issue, *biweekly* can also mean *twice a week*, which means the opportunity of being misunderstood is very real. It's always safest to spell out exactly what you mean and not rely on another's interpretation. Isn't English fun?

10. bring   action toward someone or something (v)

     take   action away from someone or something (v)

To **take** one million dollars away from Las Vegas, you have to **bring** five million to the casino when you arrive.

11. can   to have the ability to do something (v)

     may   to have the possibility or permission to do something (v)

You **may** climb the highest mountain if you **can** tolerate the height and cold.

Aha! Here's another set of words that needs a little amplification. In formal English we make a distinction between *may* and *can*. In our day we were taught to say, "May I have another imaginary friend?" rather than, "Can I . . . ?" The feeling was that *may* expressed permission, while *can* equated the ability. Back then, if a young girl asked, "Can I wear lipstick?" the answer would likely be, "You can, but you may not." Then there would be a silent look of triumph passed between all the adults within hearing distance. Take that, kid! Gotcha!

Today that fine distinction exists, but it's not nearly as strictly enforced. "Can I . . . ?" is usually answered by, "Yes, you can," or "No, you can't." The manner mavens might shudder in dismay, but the reality of the twenty-first century is that many of these so-called niceties are falling by the wayside, and you *can* say anything you want. In this case, maybe that's not so bad.

12. capital	seat of government; wealth; net worth (n); involving death penalty; extremely serious; first rate; uppercase letter (adj)
capitol	legislative or government buildings, specifically the U.S. Capitol (n)

When **capitol** begins with a **capital** letter, it refers to the building, the U.S. **Capitol**, in which the U.S. Congress meets or the surrounding area, **Capitol Hill**, in Washington, D.C., our nation's **capital**.

Heads Up 🔆

Capitol is another of the myriad words with multiple meanings that torment those learning English. Depending on the dictionary you use, there are anywhere between fourteen and twenty-three definitions of *capitol* and *capital.* What you need to remember is that **OnLy** when you're talking about government buildings, the U.S. Capit**OL**, or the Capit**OL** Hill area surrounding it will the word end in **OL**. **AL**l other usages will end in **AL**.

---

13. choose	to pick—in the present (v)
chose	picked—in the past (v)

Unfortunately, I was allowed to **choose** my piece of chocolate only after my sister **chose** hers.

14. cite   to quote from a source (v)

     site   a place, either on earth or the Internet (n)

To support her thesis on the Great Chicago Fire, Edwinna **cited** the **website** of an organization dedicated to preserving the **site** of Mrs. O'Leary's cowshed.

15. climactic   refers to the high point, or culmination (adj)

     climatic   refers to the weather (adj)

Despite the **climatic** conditions—the blizzard never let up—we got to the arena in time for the **climactic** moment when they awarded Best in Show to the Chihuahua.

16. complement   something that completes, or makes perfect (n)

     compliment   praise (n)

The commentator's **compliments** were the perfect **complement** to a nearly flawless performance.

17. compose   to form—the parts compose the whole (v)

     comprise   to include—the whole comprises the parts (v)

The alphabet **comprises** twenty-six letters that are used to **compose** all of the words in the English language.

18. conscience   sense of morality (n)
     conscious   aware (adj)

Pinocchio got into trouble when he wasn't **conscious** of his **conscience**, Jiminy Cricket.

19. convince   to create or change a belief (use with *of*) (v)
     persuade   to motivate to take an action (use with *to*) (v)

First I'm going to **convince** you of my honesty, and then I'm going to **persuade** you to buy into my time-share on Mars.

20. desert   a dry, sandy area (n)
     dessert   a sweet dish at the end of a meal (n)

After battling the **desert** sandstorm, the sheik served a refreshing ice cream **dessert**.

Hint: we tend to think of dessert as having more calories than desert sand, so it has an extra *s*. Works for us. Maybe it'll work for you, too.

21. discreet   circumspect, judicious (adj)
     discrete   separate, individual, each and every (adj)

The ingénue hoped every **discrete** critic in the audience would be **discreet** about her fall into the orchestra pit.

22. e.g.   for example (from Latin, *exempli gratia*, "for the sake of example")
    i.e.   that is, as when expanding or clarifying a definition (from Latin, *id est*)

Laura's friends (Karen, Craig, James, and John) want to see a "real" (**i.e.**, professional) hockey game—**e.g.**, the Black Hawks versus the Red Wings.

K.D.'s Proofreading Perspective

Notice that the abbreviations *i.e.* and *e.g.* always include periods, as shown. And just like the words they stand in for, when you use *i.e.* and *e.g.*, they're always followed by a comma.

23. ensure   to make certain (v)
    insure   to obtain insurance; to guarantee protection or safety (v)

To **ensure** that none of the *Survivor* contestants was unprotected, the show's producers paid a fortune to **insure** them with Pago Pago Life and Health.

Here again it's only fair to acknowledge that the two words have become interchangeable in everyday usage and therefore acknowledged as synonyms in some dictionaries.

We prefer to err on the side of tradition. Now that you know the difference between them, you can choose your own path.

24. everyday   routine, ordinary, happening daily (adj)
      every day   each day (adj + n)

Every day, in a dozen instances, the contestants realized that being in danger was going to be an **everyday** possibility.

K.D.'s Proofreading Perspective

Several years ago, Toyota had a TV campaign based on the slogan "Toyota Everyday." Knowing that they were using *everyday* incorrectly, I thought I would let them know. It turned out they actually knew that they were *grammatically* incorrect, but they had done extensive research and made a conscious decision to use one word instead of two because the focus group said they preferred one word from a *visual* perspective. What an example of usage being adapted to the target audience at the expense of accuracy. Not sure I agree with them, but, hey, I don't think it hurt them any.

25. fact   something absolutely true (n)
      factoid   conjecture masquerading as fact (n)

When we treat a **factoid** as if it were an irrefutable truth, we are putting opinion ahead of **fact**.

We included this pair of words because we so often hear *factoid* treated as if it were a tiny fact instead of an idea that may or may not have validity. Remember, the suffix *-oid* means "like" or "resembling," so just as *android* means "resembling a human" and *humanoid* means "having human qualities," *factoid* means "resembling a truth." We know popular usage is already destroying this distinction. Too bad!

26. farther   at a greater distance (adv)
    further   in addition to (adv)

After **further** studying the distance between Mars and Venus, men learned they were **farther** away from understanding women than they thought.

27. faze   to disturb or disconcert (v)
    phase   a period or cycle (n)

The **phases** of the moon have been proven to **faze** werewolves both in Transylvania and abroad.

28. flair   a special talent (n)
    flare   a sudden bright light, or an outward spread (n, v)

In the spotlight's **flare**, the ballerina's tutu **flared** around her, as she spun across the stage on her toes, demonstrating her special **flair** for the dance.

29. flaunt   to show something off (v)
    flout   to ignore or disdain (v)

Flaunting his musical style, Eminem **flouted** the conventional wisdom that white men can't rap.

30. flier   one who flies (n)
    flyer   an advertising circular (n)

After circling the globe, the solo **flier** arrived at the airport expecting a hero's welcome, only to be handed a **flyer** extolling the benefits of Sam's Crop Dusting School.

31. home (in)   to zero in on a target (v)
    hone   to sharpen (v)

After years of **honing** her skills, the archer accurately **homed in** on her target, the Olympic Gold Medal.

32. imply   to hint or suggest without actually saying (v)
    infer   to deduce from what has been said (v)

While the politician **implied** that her opponent is a crook, I **inferred** that she was worried about her own reputation.

The secret with *imply* and *infer* is that the speaker or writer *implies*, and the listener or reader *infers*. It's really no more complicated than that.

33. its   belonging to it (adj)
    it's   contraction of *it is* (pr + v)

It's impossible to stress this too often because **its** usage is so frequently incorrect.

If you can substitute *it is* for *its*, you're missing the apostrophe. If you can't make that substitution, then *its* is correct and properly shows possession.

34. later   afterward (adv)
     latter   the second of two things (n)

When ordering an appetizer and an entrée, the **latter** always arrives **later** than the former.

Latter only works when two people or things are mentioned. When there are more than two, then you should say *last* instead of *latter*.

35. lay   to place or put down (v)
     lie   to recline (v)

After she **lay** the coverlet on the bed, Grandma would **lie** down for an afternoon nap.

Here we get into transitive versus intransitive verbs, which we discussed in Chapter 5. It's one of those topics you should be aware of but not lose sleep over.

Let's give you the short version. *Lay* is a transitive verb, so it requires a direct object—e.g., the hen *laid* an egg (*egg* is the direct object). You have to *lay* something (the direct object) somewhere.

Lie is an intransitive verb, which means it has no direct object—e.g., I wanted to *lie* down. *Lie* is followed by an adverb, so you *lie down*, *lie across*, *lie over*, *lie under*, *lie in*— and we're not lying. (Don't go there—you'll get confused.)

36. less   a smaller amount (adj)
    fewer   a smaller number of persons or things (adj)

Because the marathon raised **less** money than last year, it meant **fewer** dollars would go to the individual participants.

Remember, *less* refers to uncountable amounts and *fewer* refers to things that can be enumerated. Most grocery stores haven't figured that out. If you only have a handful of items, you're directed to the checkout for "10 Items or *Less*." When we have the time and energy, we'll start pointing it out to store managers so they'll change it. Yeah. Sure they will.

37. lets   allows (v)
    let's   contraction of *let us* (v + pr)

Let's go to the Cineplex on Main Street, which **lets** us bring in our own snacks.

This is very much like *its* and *it's*. If you can replace *lets us* with *allows us to*, then you don't use the apostrophe. The easiest way to be certain is to always dispense with the verb contraction and see if it makes sense, as in, "*Let us* go to the movies."

38. loose   not tight (adj)
    lose   to fail to win (v)

If your saddle cinch is **loose**, you may fall off the horse and **lose** the race.

We can't figure out why this is so difficult for so many people, but it seems to be. The vagaries of English pronunciation give both words the same vowel sound, even though they're not spelled the same way. Keep in mind that both *lost* and *lose* have only one *o*, so if you *lose* you have lost. Don't play fast and loose with these words.

Oops! 💥

A *New York Daily News* headline asked, "Lizzie's ladies on the lose?" Since it was a story about getting around town and not dieting, we could only assume another writer and copyeditor fell into the *loose/lose* abyss.

| 39. | nauseated | to feel sick to one's stomach (v) |
| | nauseous | causes nausea (adj) |

The ice dancer was **nauseated** by his partner's **nauseous** perfume.

How often have you heard someone say, "I feel nauseous"? What that means is, "I cause nausea," which may be true but probably not what the person was trying to convey. However, once again usage has raised its head and the definitions are becoming blurred. Some dictionaries now allow *nauseous* to be used in place of *nauseated.* The only absolute rule in English is that the language will continue to change.

40. passed   past tense of *pass* (v)
    past   the time before the present (n, adj, adv)

Several times during the **past** hour, the server **passed** by with the hors d'oeuvres tray, but it was always empty.

41. predominant   prevailing (adj)
    predominate   to exert control over (v)

The **predominant** theory holds that parents still **predominate** over their children; however, that may be changing.

42. principal   person in charge; interest earning money or debt (n); primary or most important (adj)
    principle   rule or ethical standard (n)

Her **principal** task was to uphold the **principles** on which the school was founded, and **Principal** Snodgrass did just that.

43. prostate   male reproductive gland (n)
    prostrate   to bow down in a submissive position (v); helpless; prone (adj)

Eldon was **prostrate** with grief after he received the diagnosis of **prostate** cancer.

Most women have listened patiently while a man talked about his *prostrate*, all the while wondering why the poor darling didn't know the correct name for his own anatomy. Once and for all, guys, your *prostate* gland has only one *r*.

44. sensual	refers to bodily appetites and passions (adj)
sensuous	delight in beautiful things (adj)
sexual	having or involving sex (adj)

The **sensuous** pleasure he took in looking at a beautiful sunset was quite different from his **sensual** enjoyment of food or the **sexual** satisfaction he found at home.

| 45. stationary | not moving (adj) |
| stationery | paper (n) |

Working out on the **stationary** bike, Percival pushed the pedals and wished for a piece of **stationery** so he could write his mother.

| 46. than | compares (conj) |
| then | subsequent action (adv) |

At the ski lodge, nothing is better **than** a hot cup of cocoa in front of the fire, **then** later snuggling under a warm comforter for a good night's sleep.

47. their   possessive of *they* (pr)
    there   in that place (n, adv)
    they're   contraction of *they are* (pr + v)

"**There** is no place like home," **their** mother always said, and now **they're** at an age where they agree with her.

48. to   toward (prep)
    too   also (prep); extremely (adv)
    two   more than one and less than three (n, adj)

The **two** gremlins, up **to** no good, went **to** great lengths to make sure everyone else got in trouble, **too**, because it was **too** difficult for them to behave differently.

49. who's   contraction of *who is* or *who has* (pr + v)
    whose   possessive form of who (adj)

"**Whose** bike is in the driveway?" Dad yelled. "And **who's** going to pick up the pieces and put them away?"

50. your   belonging to you (adj)
    you're   contraction of *you are* (pr + v)

By this point, **your** head is full of right and wrong usages, and **you're** probably wondering what comes next.

Ten Word Choices You Make Regularly

Now that we've given you fifty sets of words that are commonly misused, let's look at ten other word choices that can make us stop and think for a minute.

A *or* An?

We all know that you use *a* before a word beginning with a consonant and *an* before a word beginning with a vowel, so it's *a* pear and *an* apple, but what about words beginning with an *h*? What do you use before them? In American English, we use *a* if you pronounce the *h* and *an* if you don't. It's *a* hotel but *an* hour.

When you're dealing with acronyms or abbreviations, consider how the first letter is pronounced. It's *a* CIA agent, *an* FBI official, *a* U.S. senator, *an* ICBM missile, etc.

Awhile *or* a While?

Here's a case where the meaning is absolutely the same. You simply have two ways of expressing it that are equally correct, *if* you remember one point: *awhile* means "for a time," and *a while* means "a time." So if you write, "I'll be on vacation for awhile," what you're actually saying is, "I'll be on vacation for for a time," which sounds silly and makes the grammar checker in your word processing program go crazy.

Correct: After checking out who else was at the party, Truman decided **to stay awhile** and enjoy himself.

Correct: It had been **a while** since he had allowed himself time off to have fun.

Incorrect: Gertrude told him if he stayed for **awhile** longer they could leave together.

Bad *or* Badly*?*

It all depends on whether you're describing the condition of the subject or the action itself. In other words, are you using the adjective or the adverb?

Bad is an adjective and adjectives describe nouns. Subjects are either nouns or pronouns. So if you want to describe the subject, use an adjective.

Correct: The clown **felt bad** that no one laughed when he fell off the trapeze.

Incorrect: The clown **felt badly** that no one laughed when he fell off the trapeze.

Badly is an adverb, so it describes verbs (actions), not nouns. If you want to describe how an action is performed, you need an adverb.

Correct: The clown knew he'd **performed badly** because people didn't laugh.

Hanged *or* Hung?

The rule here is pretty clear-cut. People are *hanged* by the neck until dead. Posters are *hung* on the walls of every dorm in America.

Hung is also an adjective, referring to the inability to reach a decision or verdict.

> The museum walls **were hung** with one famous painting after another.

> The defendant **hanged** himself after his trial ended with a **hung** jury.

Like *or* As (As If)?

These can be tricky. In casual speech and writing, *like* is gaining ground. But to be absolutely correct, stick to the following rules.

To compare two things, use *like* before nouns that don't have verbs.

> *Correct:* The gladiator strode into the amphitheater **like a conquering hero**.

> *Incorrect (for same meaning):* The gladiator strode into the amphitheater **as a conquering hero**.

In the preceding example, changing *like* to *as* changes the meaning entirely. In the first sentence, the probably petrified gladiator is projecting the air of a conquering hero. In the second sentence, if he actually *were* a conquering hero, fresh from his achievement, he wouldn't be fighting lions to keep Nero from fiddling around.

To compare two things when a verb is involved, use *as* or *as if*.

> *Correct:* The games began at noon, just **as they had** the day before.

> *Incorrect:* The games began at noon, just **like they had** the day before.

> *Correct:* He fought the lions **as if** his life depended on it; it did.

> *Incorrect:* He fought the lions **like** his life depended on it; it did.

Of course, if you listen to some young people speak, like you'd think *like* was like a word to use almost like Toni uses commas, like it's OK to like say it like all the time. Like, why not? Read those last two sentences aloud and, like, don't ask "Why not?" again!

Lighted *or* Lit?

This one's for Toni because it's one of her pet peeves. Back in the "old days," it was never correct to say, "she lit the lamp." *Lit* was strictly a slang term for insobriety, and the lamp was always *lighted*. Once, when seeing the offending *lit* in her daughter's third grade textbook, she asked the teacher about it. The young woman had no idea it was a new usage, so Toni said, "I'm delit it doesn't bother you."

Now obviously, times have changed and water has flowed under the bridge and it's silly to assume English won't have as many exceptions as it has rules. *Light* and *delight* certainly can't be expected to convert to the past tense in the same way. Today *lit* and *lighted* are both correct, but *lighted* remains more elegant—and, at least to Toni, it just sounds better!

Specially *or* Especially?

These two adverbs are close in meaning—so close that many dictionaries give identical definitions. But to some of us there remains a subtle distinction between the two. *Specially* is used when referring to a definite purpose or way of doing something.

> The costume **was specially made** for Spiderman.

> The wine steward **specially selected** a bottle of Château Lafite Rothschild Pauillac 1996 to please the connoisseur.

Especially has a double usage. First, it can be used as a synonym for *in particular* or *particularly*.

> Millions of viewers, **especially women**, watched the royal wedding.

Especially can also be used to intensify what you're saying.

> While the entire dinner was a gourmet's delight, the chocolate soufflé was **especially delectable**.

This is another case in which you won't be drummed out of the regiment if you confuse the two words. It's the rare person who'll call you on it. But isn't it fun to know you're using the words especially well?

Until *or* Till?

Here's the good news—again, you can take your pick. *Until* and *till* are equally correct and virtually interchangeable. Please notice there's no apostrophe in either word.

However, we also see the variations *'til* and *'till*. Both of those are incorrect, wrong, and never to be used. Period. End of discussion.

Which *or* That?

In American English, when a clause begins with *that*, it is never set off by commas. The clause introduces information essential to the meaning of the sentence.

> The article **that** he filed yesterday went unpublished. (But the one he filed the day before was on the front page.)

The clause starting with *that* specifies which report we're talking about.

Which begins clauses that are set off by commas because it introduces information considered only supplementary to the meaning of the sentence.

> The article, **which** he filed yesterday, went unpublished.

There's only one report, so no need to specify which one. The clause starting with *which* is just extra information.

Who *or* Whom?

Obviously this is a real sore point with us, so please indulge us as we give it a quick review. You will know whether to use *who* or *whom* before we're done!

Who is always the subject. *Whom* is always the object. Our advice, when in doubt about *whom*, is to rewrite the sentence or just drop it altogether. Usually, you don't need it, and if you use it incorrectly, you'll sound either clueless or affected.

Please don't feel you're alone in your confusion. Here is an example of how not to use it from a well-recognized source.

Oops! ✳

"We focus on who's sleeping **with who**, but miss who you are really with." (Angelina Jolie)

Correct: We focus on who's sleeping **with whom**, but miss who you are really with.

It's apparent that the *who/whom* confusion isn't going to go away anytime soon. Keep in mind that *who does something to whom* and you'll always be correct.

Four Words to Never or Rarely Use

The four words discussed next—two of which are used constantly but shouldn't be, and two that crop up in speech like dandelions on a summer lawn—are all better off left out of your vocabulary.

Actually

OK, you could use the intensifier *actually* on rare occasions, but basically it has become almost as annoying as *like* in everyday speech because some people drop it in after every few words.

> **Actually**, I did have a date for the prom, but he **actually** stood me up, so **actually**, I had to go with my brother.

To correct that sentence, drop out every *actually*.

Another consideration is that dropping *actually* (or *truthfully* or *really* or *honestly*) into your conversation implies that everything else you've said isn't so *actual*, *truthful*, *real*, or *honest*. If you always speak the truth, and of course you do, why would you point it out in this instance?

So when you need to pump up the intensity of your argument, the occasional *actually* might work, but we'd prefer you just rewrite the sentence.

Alright

This word has fallen into the language for no good reason. It shouldn't be used. Instead, say *all right*.

It's **all right** to be informal or use slang, if you use it correctly and appropriately.

The only time you hyphenate the words is when they are part of a compound adjective.

Batman was an **all-right guy**, if you like people who sleep hanging upside down.

Irregardless

Here's another "do not use" entry, although we hear it all the time, which is a little scary to us.

The prefix *ir-* means "not." The suffix *-less* means "without." Thus it follows that *regardless* means "without regard." Add *ir-* to it and you have "not without regard," or a double negative, which is, of course, a positive, so you're not saying what you want to anyway. Confusing? Doesn't have to be. Just drop *irregardless* from your vocabulary. You'll do fine without it—and so will your readers or listeners.

Very

Here's a case of overusage taking the starch out of a word. *Very* is a valid intensifier, but when it's used in one sentence after another, it no longer imparts the punch you're looking for.

The American author and humorist Mark Twain wrote, "Substitute *damn* every time you're inclined to write *very*; your editor will delete it and the writing will be just as it should be."

That advice is as sound today as it was in the 1800s.

Ten Rules You'll Want to Know About Word Choices 🍂

A quick review of the following rules every once in a while should keep you humming along and using the right word in the right place at the right time:

1. With the verbs *to effect/affect*, use *effect* when you mean to accomplish and *affect* when you mean to influence.

2. *Dessert* has more calories than a *desert*, so it has a double helping of the letter *s*.

3. The suffix *-oid* means "like" or "resembling," so just as *android* means "resembling a human," a *factoid* means "resembling a truth."

4. The secret to keeping *imply* and *infer* straight is that the speaker or writer *implies*, and the listener or reader *infers*.

5. When you're unsure about *its/it's* or *lets/let's*, read the verb without contracting it and see if the sentence makes sense.

6. *Lay* requires a direct object (*lay* the DVD on the table), and *lie* requires an adverb (set the alarm before you *lie* down for a nap).

7. *Less* refers to uncountable amounts, and *fewer* refers to things that can be enumerated (*less* income results in *fewer* purchases).

8. *Bad* is an adjective that describes a person, place, or thing; *badly* is an adverb that describes an action.

9. When choosing between *hanged* and *hung*, remember that a person is *hanged* and curtains are *hung*.

10. Avoid using *alright* or *irregardless*, and use *actually* and *very* only on rare occasions.

VIVID VOCABULARY AND SUPERIOR SPELLING

IT'S IMPOSSIBLE to speak a language without words, and while we take them for granted, our vocabulary words—and the way we spell them—tell a lot about us. In this chapter we're going to pay attention to the words that make up our sentences, how we use them, why we shouldn't use some of them, and how to spell those we do use.

How Important Is Your Vocabulary?

Most people want to increase their vocabulary, which explains why the *Reader's Digest* monthly feature "It Pays to Increase Your Word Power" has been running since 1945.

There's a long-running advertisement for a vocabulary enhancement program in which the announcer intones,

"People judge you by the words you use." The program promises to teach you words that will mark you as educated and intelligent—but also incomprehensible to most people you talk to.

Our mantra is that language is a communications tool. If the people you're speaking to or writing for don't understand you, the whole purpose of language has been nullified. Your vocabulary, at least those words you use every day, should be readily understood by everyone around you. If they're not, you need to tailor your language so your vocabulary is understood. Otherwise, why speak at all?

According to the best estimates, there are about a half million words in the English language. If you add in all the scientific terms, you'd have another half million. Etymologist Dave Wilton, who has written widely on the origins of words and phrases, estimates that the second edition of the *Oxford English Dictionary* has 290,000 entries with more than 600,000 word forms. By comparison, German, which is the root language of English, has about 185,000 words. Even with our Germanic base, the English language is filled with words that have their origins in Latin, Greek, Italian, French, Spanish, and a wealth of other languages. When you take into account all the borrowing of words that has gone on, it's easy to see why English is one of the richest and most diverse of all the world's languages.

Given that embarrassment of resources on which to draw, think of this. If you're a typical educated American, you know about 20,000 English words. Of those, some are scatological or obscene (come on, admit it—we all know the basic four-letter words), and some are slang or region specific. Then there are the approximately 2,000 words you use most every day. And the rest are words you recognize but don't bother with unless you run into them accidentally.

Making it even harder to keep current, Jeff Davidson of the Breathing Space Institute reports that 66,000 new words were added to our language between 1964 and 2004. That's more than half of the 100,000 words estimated to be in the French language. There's no way any English speaker is going to know every word in the dictionary.

Add to that the words common to the sciences and law and you really have to scramble just to keep up. Lawyers have a special vocabulary even when they're not using legal Latin. In 1994 a juror in the Rodney King trial in Los Angeles was severely reprimanded for sneaking a dictionary into the trial. She wanted to know the meaning of the word *reprehensible*. The judge ruled that she hadn't damaged the case and deliberations could proceed, but he said, "The introduction of extraneous material is very serious." A dictionary? Extraneous material? Would we rather our jurors don't understand what they're hearing? That's a discussion for another time and place. The point here is that there should never be shame or reprimand for making sure what a word really means. If you need to carry a dictionary in your pocket, go for it. We're cheering you on.

Choosing Your Words

So how do we choose which vocabulary to use and which to ignore? There's no easy answer to that one. If you're a wordsmith, someone who thoroughly enjoys working with words and who considers word games great fun, you'll gladly take on the challenge of learning at least one new word a day.

Even if you're not that fascinated, you can brush up your basic vocabulary so that you are using interesting new words in creative ways.

One caveat: be sure you know the meaning of the word you're using. It doesn't enhance your image if you're using the word incorrectly or mispronouncing it. With a good dictionary, it's not difficult to make certain you know what a word really means, how it's used, and how it's pronounced. You'll find that some of the online dictionaries include an audio option that allows you to hear the word pronounced correctly.

Spelling is a little trickier. If you don't realize that *pneumonia* starts with a silent *p* or that *mnemonic* begins with a silent *m*, you're going to have trouble looking them up in the dictionary. Spell-checkers or the Internet can help, but as we'll point out later, they can also be next to useless in many situations. We certainly use ours with fair regularity, but no machine can replace a good dictionary close at hand. Type in your approximation of the word, and your word processing program may give you the correct spelling. On search engines, you'll often see that somewhat snide inquiry "Did you mean . . . ?"

In the mid-1980s, Chicago mayor Harold Washington was constantly at war with various opposing factions. His assessment of those he perceived as wrongdoers was that they were "scurrilous." They were spreading unfair or false criticism that would damage someone's reputation, namely his. People were scurrilous. Situations were scurrilous. Criticisms of him were scurrilous. To this day, we wonder how many people hearing him declaim the latest perceived unfairness knew what he was saying. Perhaps it's better to be remembered for what you really said instead of what people didn't understand you meant.

New Words

New words enter the language regularly. It's fun to watch them arrive, take root, and become part of the landscape. In the past few years we've added many, often thanks to the Internet. Who would have thought we would read an *e-zine* (online magazine) or a *blog* (online journal), complain about *spam* (unwanted e-mail) or *phishing* (scam e-mails sent to obtain information for identity theft), or consider ourselves a *surfing netizen* (an avid Internet user)? There's at least one website (of course there is) dedicated to defining all the new Internet words so the neophyte and techie alike can stay current with the ever-changing terminology (netlingo.com).

There are also words that reenter the language. *Pleather* (plastic leather) appeared in the *Merriam-Webster's* dictionary for the first time in 2004, but it was first used in 1982. Back in 2000, while the country held its breath waiting for the last *chad* to drop in Florida, we wondered where we got that word for the punched-out piece of a ballot. Actually, it came about in the 1940s when the wastebaskets of teletype operators were piled high with chads, the pieces of paper punched out to make machine-readable holes in paper and punch cards. As the song lyric says, "Everything old is new again."

We have a highly unscientific theory that when you run across a new word, if you look it up and learn its meaning, you'll find yourself very quickly running into it over and over again. Back in the 1970s, a coworker put a note on Toni's desk with nothing but the word *omphaloskepsis* written on it. Toni finally had to call the Chicago Public Library Q & A service to find out it was a noun describing the contemplation of one's navel. Who would ever use that word again? *The New York Times*, for one. It appeared in that Sunday's crossword puzzle. It was also in the next month's issue of *Games* magazine, where the editorial column was headlined "Omphaloskepsis Anyone?" She's only seen it once or twice since, but she'll never forget it.

The obvious question is whether the new word has always been right under our noses and we just bounced over it like a nasty pothole in the road, or is there some harmony in the spheres that reinforces it for us at a particular time? As much as we'd like to espouse the latter, we're pretty sure we just ignore an unfamiliar word until there's a reason to add it to our vocabulary.

K.D.'s Tidbit

My mom, Ann Longknife, Ph.D., teaches English and Critical Thinking at a junior college. To build vocabulary, she, of course, encourages her students to read, read, read. She also suggests they carry a small address book. Since not everyone carries around a dictionary, she tells them that when they are reading something and come to a word they don't know, they should jot it down in the small address book (under the letter that the word starts with). Then when they do have access to a dictionary, they should look it up. What a great idea!

A recent addition to the common language is the word *schadenfreude*, a word from German meaning to take pleasure in another's misfortune (*Schaden*—"harm," *Freude*—"joy"). In the late 1990s, it showed up in magazines like *The New Yorker*, always in italics, as editors are wont to do when a word might be foreign or unfamiliar although not always defined in the text. Gradually, the italics disappeared. Newspapers picked up the word, using it in the sports pages and political editorials. In 2000, *Newsweek* ran a story headlined "Silicon Valley's Latest Craze: Schadenfreude—The German concept of rejoicing in the misfortunes of others is thriving in the ruins of the New Economy." About six months later, the *San Francisco Chronicle* ran a headline over an article about the Internet bust: "Pack up the schadenfreude." Finally, the word made its way to the comic pages. An "Enjoy Your Schadenfreude" greeting card can't be far behind.

It undoubtedly became popular because it's a great word that nails an emotion most of us have been guilty of at one time or another. That said, should you use it in everyday language? Probably not, at least not without some sort of follow-up explanation. Just because a word has crept into print doesn't mean everyone will have seen it—or taken the time to look it up. We're willing to bet that the vast majority of people have never heard the word despite the more than a quarter million citations (or is that site-ations?) on Google. But it is fun to know it and to enjoy the schadenfreude when someone else is clueless and misses the point altogether.

Grammar writer James Kilpatrick talks about using new vocabulary as "indulging yourself with a gloriously unfamiliar word" and compares it to a pitcher throwing a different pitch into the mix to keep the batter alert. But he warns, "Remember that too many hard words eventually will repel more readers than they attract." William Safire, in his book *Fumblerules*, admonishes, "Never use a long word when a diminutive one will do." Good advice, even when delivered tongue-in-cheek.

We would never say you shouldn't use and enjoy new words. The issue is this: if your listeners or readers don't recognize the word you're using, it immediately puts them on the defensive. They feel stupid, not up to par, and probably a little embarrassed. That's the last thing you want. Instead of making a point, you've lost your point of connection.

The standard level for comprehension in the United States is pegged at tenth grade level, although military manuals and most product instructions are closer to sixth grade level. Think of high school sophomores you know. Would they understand what you're saying? Until you're sure of your audience, keep your vocabulary sweet and simple. It will pay off in the long run.

Foreign Words

The New York Times' writers seem to delight in using language guaranteed to make the most fervent wordie stop and think, but in the sentence below one outdid himself. Discussing a restaging of Ibsen's *Hedda Gabler*, the reviewer got carried away. Take this sentence (please!), "Liberatingly, you come to think of Hedda not as a sui generis exotic, that evil Scandinavian cat, but as a character with a context and a persuasive raison d'être." Let's see—we have an awkward adverb (*liberatingly*), a Latin reference (*sui generis*—"being the only one of its kind"), and a French phrase (*raison d'être*—"reason for being") all mucked about in a sentence that doesn't make much sense.

Where was the editor to turn the words around and restore the language to English? Perhaps something like "It's liberating to think of Hedda not as some Scandinavian breed of cat, exotic and evil, but as a character who has both a context and a persuasive reason to exist."

As much pride as we took in declaring our independence, we Americans love to drop foreign references and phrases into our language. They are perceived to add a certain spice to otherwise bland speech. If we can figure out how, we casually drop *c'est la vie* (that's life), *du jour* (today's special), *n'est-ce pas?* (isn't it so?), *mañana* (tomorrow), *comme ci, comme ça* (so-so), and *déjà vu* (already seen), and let's not forget *ad infinitum* (eternal) and its cousin *ad nauseam* (to the point of making one sick).

Too often we hear some version of Sam Goldwyn's comment, "It's déjà vu all over again." That's repetitively redundant. If you want to drop foreign phrases into your vocabulary, go for it—*chacun à son goût* (each to his own taste)—but realize that you may be way over the head of your audience.

You have our *carte blanche* (permission) to utter *bon mots* (witty remarks), even *sotto voce* (in a low voice), as long as you don't become an *enfant terrible* (outrageously outspoken person), a *bête noire* (someone disliked) whose presence is *verboten* (prohibited) in the *beau monde* (high society) because you use foreign terms *ad absurdum* (to the point of absurdity). Use a little discretion, *por favor* (please).

Heads Up

The following words are just a few of those we commonly use that require foreign accents, known as diacritics:

à la	crème
attaché	crêpe
bric-a-brac	crudités
café	décor
canapé	déjà vu
cause célèbre	derrière
château	El Niño (La Niña)
cliché	entrée
consommé	exposé
coup d'état	façade

fiancé (fiancée)	piñata
ingénue	protégé (protégée)
jalapeño	purée
maître d'	résumé
mañana	sauté
ménage à trois	soirée
né (née)	touché
passé	über-
pâté	vis-à-vis
piña colada	voilà

And here are five common phrases that use words with diacritics:

Bon appétit!
Comme ci, comme ça.
Hasta mañana.
La crème de la crème.
¿Qué pasa?

Slang

If you've ever studied a foreign language and then visited that country only to find yourself unable to understand what the natives are saying, a good share of your confusion can probably be traced to slang. Every language has its own slang words and phrases, which usually are not taught in school. For that matter, every generation uses slang terms not generally found outside that age group. When a foreigner says he or she can't understand *Variety* magazine, the venerable chronicler of the Hollywood entertainment industry, it's because *Variety* is very slangy. It came up with this famous headline when the market crashed in 1929: "Wall Street Lays an Egg." And it coined *payola* in a 1938 headline, "Plug Payolas Perplexed." When nonnative English speakers read headlines like "The Lion in Whimper" or "Studios Mining Moppet Mania," they're rightfully confused. Sometimes we are, too.

Teenagers of any generation have their own slang. Our advice: don't try and gain their confidence by attempting to speak their language, which is in perpetual flux. You'll only prove that you're older than dirt and totally not clued in.

Advertisers take a chance when they use slang in ads. A recent Mercedes-Benz magazine insert blares "Get the 411"—current slang for information because it's the number we dial on the phone for that purpose. Will the magazine's usually older, more affluent customer base get it? Only its ad agency will know for sure.

Thanks to the Internet, it's become more common to be asked for your *coordinates* when someone wants your contact information. It may sound hip and high tech, but it does make humans sound like satellites.

Our advice is to omit slang completely when talking to anyone whose native language isn't English, at least until you've had an opportunity to see how comfortable they are with it.

Heads Up

Speaking English to nonnative speakers can be a challenge, whether or not you pepper it with foreign terms. The way to get through to someone who's not totally conversant in your language isn't to speak louder. Instead, simplify your words and sentence structure.

The Problems with Mondegreens and Homophones

Mondegreens are those mistaken song lyrics, catchphrases, slogans, and such that are misheard or misunderstood, often hilariously, and then repeated in the erroneous version. There used to be a joke about the Mexican immigrant who went to an American baseball game to celebrate his new resident status. When he got home, he called his mother in Guadalajara and announced, "The Americans are so glad that I'm a citizen that they want me to be happy, so before the game everyone stood up and sang, 'José, can you see?'" That's a mondegreen. Another would be singing "Lucy in the Sky with Diamonds" as "Lucy in Disguise with Diamonds."

Toni had a client who was very upset with the way his business was running. During a long phone call, during which he ranted on about his partner's perceived double-dealing, he repeatedly asked, "Does he think I just fell off a turned-up truck?" He obviously hadn't heard about the *turnip truck*.

What happens too often is we hear regular vocabulary words incorrectly and incorporate them into our speech. One friend didn't recognize the difference between *cavalry* and *Calvary* until it was gently pointed out that soldiers on horseback didn't equate to the site of the Crucifixion.

Too often we want to incorporate fancy-sounding words into our vocabulary, only to find out down the line that we incorporated the wrong word. One business associate said, "The problem was *exasperated* [frustrated] by corporate intervention," instead of "*exacerbated* [made worse]." It's easy to make the mistake. It's equally easy to fix it so you don't make it again. If you're unsure, look up the word. Make very certain you heard correctly the first time and you're repeating it in the correct context.

Homophones are words that sound alike but mean different things—for instance, *fair/fare*, *bare/bear*, *pray/prey*, *tail/tale*, *cereal/serial*, *boulder/bolder*, *tied/tide*, *sweet/suite*, *grown/groan*, *knight/night*, and so on. Despite our best efforts, most of us occasionally use the wrong word when writing, probably because there's been a momentary glitch in a synapse. At least we hope that's all it is.

This is just a reminder to be careful. Sometimes reading a passage *aloud* (not *allowed*) will point out the misspelling. There was an Olympic athlete who was initially angry because he thought the sportscaster predicted he'd "meddle in Atlanta" instead of "medal in Atlanta." In print, there wouldn't have been any confusion.

Oops! ✹

This sentence came out of *First*, a leading women's magazine:

"The family was already putting the **breaks** on their shared memory making with each passing year."

Those are the *brakes*!

Spelling—It's Not All That Difficult

It doesn't take great intelligence to spell correctly because you can look up any word—and if you can't find a particular word, maybe that's a clue it isn't really a word. (Actually, Toni hopes it's a sign of genius when she invents alternate spellings.) Spelling does take attention to detail and a concern about how you look in print.

Unfortunately, we *are* judged by the way we spell. The fine art of putting letters in the correct order to form a specific word has fallen into disrepair, and increasingly we're seeing really good material marred by really bad spelling errors. Send out a letter with words—and even worse, names—misspelled, and see how much positive response it generates. Toni once received a letter from a freelance writer looking for work. Not only were her first and last names misspelled (Tony Boil), but the name of the company was as well. To make things worse, there were other errors in the interior of the letter. You can bet that independent contractor remained unemployed. If potential associates see that you can't take the time to spell correctly, especially in a solicitation letter, how can they assume you'll be correct in any other part of an assignment?

K.D.'s Proofreading Perspective

In 1963, when Lands' End, the famous clothing company, produced its first printed catalog, the misplaced apostrophe was a typo. The powers that be in the company decided that at that point they couldn't afford to fix it, so they left it as is—where it's lived happily and successfully all these years.

A fun story, but we don't recommend you do this at home.

Spelling errors and bad grammar in personal ads are so common that companies have been set up to help advertising singles compose and edit their appeals for a partner. E-mails are constantly delivering funny pictures of misspelled signs—only they aren't that funny. In Los Angeles we saw a sign in front of a McDonald's that was open while undergoing renovation. Aware that there would be some inconvenience during this time, the sign asked customers to "please bare with us during construction."

K.D.'s Proofreading Perspective

OK, considering my business is editorial services, with a focus on proofreading and editing, I can't emphasize enough the importance of accurate spelling and grammar. The best thing is, of course, to learn for yourself the right way to spell, write, and speak. However, when you're preparing a written document, also ask someone else to read it for you whenever possible. Reading what you've written yourself, you tend to see what you expect to see. If you can have a professional proofreader look it over, even better.

One more comment about the quality of what you write that is representing *you*—to use one of Toni's favorite lines, "Even Hemingway had an editor." When you have something important to say, learn to say it the best you can—then don't hesitate to ask an editor or a proofreader to help you polish it up.

Back in the 1940s and '50s, a lot of educators veered away from teaching phonics and taught a flash card–driven word recognition method of reading commonly referred to as See and Say. The survivors of that training learned to read because they learned to recognize words by sight. They just didn't learn how to spell correctly because they had no phonetic background to rely on. Just ask Toni. She knows when a word looks wrong, but she doesn't always know how to fix it without resorting to the trusty dictionary.

In the mid-'50s, Rudolf Flesch wrote a book called *Why Johnny Can't Read*, in which he blamed a good share of the nation's deplorable reading scores on the look-say method. Educators made a U-turn and returned to the phonics system. However, it doesn't seem it's working very well either considering how much is misspelled these days.

The issue of how to simplify English spelling has been going on for well over a century. In the 1800s the acerbic British playwright George Bernard Shaw got into the spelling controversy. Educators and reformers were trying to standardize spelling based on existing pronunciations. Said Mr. Shaw, "That's fine but then 'fish' should be spelled 'ghoti.'" Just to tweak the noses of the academics, he would wax eloquent on the subject, explaining it this way:

F = **gh** as in enou**gh**
I = **o** as in w**o**men
SH = **ti** as in ac**ti**on

Obviously, simplifying spelling based on phonics was a crazy idea that would never have gotten off the ground, but Shaw delighted in the thought that he had something to do with its early demise.

Spelling seems to be difficult even in obvious places. In Livermore, California, a town about forty miles southeast of San Francisco, the library paid an artist $40,000 to create a ceramic tile mural set into the pavement outside the new library building. The sixteen-foot-wide installation is a tribute to prominent figures in the arts and sciences. Sounds great, but it didn't all turn out as planned. Of the 175 men and women honored on the tiles, eleven names are misspelled, including "Eistein" (should be Einstein), "Shakespere" (should be Shakespeare), "Van Gough" (should be Van Gogh), and "Michaelangelo" (should be Michelangelo). (We don't know about you, but for $40,000, we would have taken a few minutes to look up the correct spellings.)

The artist, Maria Alquilar, initially refused when asked to fix the problems but later decided she would correct them for a fee. She defended her mistakes saying, "I just wasn't that concerned. None of us are particularly good spellers anymore because of computers. When you are in a studio full of clay, you don't give it much thought." Further, she contended, real artists wouldn't have noticed the errors. "The people that are into humanities, and are into Blake's concept of enlightenment, they are not looking at the words. In their mind, the words register correctly."

That should send a shiver up your spine. As philosopher George Santayana said, "Those who ignore history are condemned to repeat it." In the same vein, those who ignore spelling errors are reinforcing them for the generations to come.

Words Most Often Misspelled

Which words send you to the dictionary most often? Chances are they're on this list. Make a copy and post it within an easy glance from where you work to avoid errors and save time.

accommodate	discipline
accumulate	embarrass
acknowledgment	entrepreneur
allotment	envelope
all right	existence
analyze	familiar
annihilate	fiery
benefit	fluorescent
bouillon	foreign
caffeine	harass
colonel	height
conscientious	hemorrhage
counterfeit	innuendo

inoculate	recommend
judgment	restaurant
liaison	rhythm
lightning	ridiculous
likelihood	separate
liquefy	siege
maintenance	silhouette
maneuver	skeptical
necessary	sophomore
niece	spaghetti
occasion	succeed
occurrence	supersede
parallel	surprise
paraphernalia	surveillance
personnel	synonymous
pneumonia	thorough
precede	tranquillity
prejudice	unanimous
privilege	usage
proceed	vacuum
process	veterinarian
questionnaire	waiver
realtor	weird
receive	withheld

Oops!

We wouldn't be us if we didn't point out that even the mighty spell-checker at Microsoft got *tranquillity* wrong. According to most dictionaries, two *l*s are preferred, although this will undoubtedly become another victim of popular usage. Maybe it's not a word they use much in software companies.

Mnemonic Methods of Spelling

Mnemonics are nothing more than ways to remember something. They can be verses like "Thirty days hath September . . ." or a sentence to recall the planets in order from the sun: "Mother Very Early Made John Some Unusually Nice Pie." Mnemonics can be a help when spelling, too.

The "*e* before *i*" or "*i* before *e*" dilemma should have been resolved when we were in school and dutifully parroted

> Use *i* before *e*
> Except after *c*
> Or when sounded like *a*
> As in *neighbor* or *weigh*.

This is a good rule to remember, but there are even more exceptions than those noted in the rhyme.

The *ie* irregulars include

ancient	society
conscience	species
glaciers	sufficient
science	

Among the *ei* exceptions are

caffeine	neither
counterfeit	protein
either	seize/seizure
foreign	sheik
forfeit	sovereign
heifer	surfeit
height	their
heir	veil
leisure	weird

It's probably safest just to commit these we*ir*d words to memory. By this point, you ought to be accustomed to the fact that the rules are constantly broken in this marvelous language of ours.

The memory devices for learning words are as varied as the people who use them.

Toni has never misspelled *cemetery* (with all *e*'s) since a teacher told her, "Everyone was at *e*'s there."

If you have trouble with spelling *rhythm*, just remember, "*R*hythm *H*elps *Y*our *T*wo *H*ips *M*ove."

To always spell *necessary* correctly (with a single *c* and double *s*), remember, "You have one collar but two socks."

Assume makes an *ass* out of *u* and *me*.

There is *a rat* in sep*arat*e, although the folks at *Consumer Reports* didn't know this when they sent out an envelope that asked, "Can you *seperate* the facts from fiction?"

K.D.'s Proofreading Perspective 🍁

A trick I still use for a few words that I can never seem to remember how to spell is to put them on a sticky note on the inside cover of my dictionary. Then at least when I do need to look them up, they're closer at hand.

You get the idea. If you have a word that's troublesome, make up a sentence or an association that will help you remember it. We've found mnemonics work best when we invent our own so we don't have to try and remember someone else's.

The Fearsome Fallacy of Spell-Check

So what are we going to do about the abysmal state of spelling today? We can see you smiling, thinking, "I've got spell-check." Well, we all have spell-check, and that's the rub. Spell-check is certainly better than nothing, but it isn't infallible and it's almost never the last word. Spell-check is where vocabulary and spelling intertwine with a vengeance.

The following verse has been around the Internet so long that it would be impossible to accurately credit it to any one person, but our hats are off to the man or woman who put it together.

> Eye halve a spelling checker
> It came with my pea sea
> It plainly marques four my revue
> Miss steaks eye kin knot sea.
> Eye strike a key and type a word
> And weight four it two say
> Weather eye am wrong oar write
> It shows me strait a weigh.
> As soon as a mist ache is maid
> It nose bee fore two long
> And eye can put the error rite
> Its rare lea ever wrong.
> Eye have run this poem threw it
> I am shore your pleased two no
> Its letter perfect in it's weigh
> My checker tolled me sew.

We shouldn't have to say much more than that. Spell-checkers can be useful tools if used properly. Rely on them exclusively though, and you, too, can write gibberish.

Of course, the problem is that spell-checkers only recognize words, not meanings. The poem shows the problem perfectly. As close as it seems to come on occasion, the computer can't think. It only reacts to a set of inputs, and it is completely oblivious to homophones. If you want to write, "All threw the game, Oswald through the ball across the plate," no spell-checker is ever going to tap you on the virtual shoulder and cough politely to indicate you goofed.

A current dictionary within arm's reach is still the best spell-checker you'll ever find.

Ten Ways to Brush Up on Your Vocabulary and Spelling Skills

Here are ten simple rules to remember to brush up your vocabulary and spelling skills:

1. It's better to be remembered for what you really said instead of what people didn't understand you meant, so speak to be understood, not to impress.
2. Don't use new words without being certain they will be understood. Doh!
3. The occasional foreign phrase adds color, but too many foreign words will turn your audience color-blind.
4. Slang is best shared with native speakers of your generation.
5. When speaking to nonnative speakers, keep your sentence structure and vocabulary simple and direct and slow down your speaking rate.
6. Mondegreens and homophones can trip up even the most experienced English speaker.

7. Taking the time to make certain that words are spelled correctly is essential if you want to be taken seriously.
8. Create simple mnemonics to help you spell difficult words correctly.
9. Never, never, never rely totally on spell-check!
10. A current dictionary close at hand is your best vocabulary and spelling tool.

A Dose of Style
Putting It All Together

ONCE YOU HAVE all the tools—the parts of speech, punctuation, vocabulary—you may be wondering how all these elements combine to make intelligible, perhaps even elegant, English. More than that, how are you going to tailor that English to your audience, be it casual or more formal or business oriented? We're going to give you some solid tips for how to do it, no matter what you're writing. Style is a combination of the words you use and the way you put those words together when you speak or write.

Get in Touch with Style

We can give you rules and regulations and *however* exceptions all day long, but what does that really tell you about style, that individual rhythm and melody of each person's language? Not much. Style is very individual. Each of us speaks and writes the language just a little differently. Toni's Italian grandmother taught her three daughters how to make spaghetti sauce. They, in turn, taught the next generation, and yet each woman makes a sauce that is unique and distinctive, all the while using the same ingredients and basically the same recipe. What individual taste does to sauce is what style does to language.

To the attuned ear, style can be compared to various musicians playing the same melody. As William Strunk, Jr., and E. B. White, the authors of *The Elements of Style*, said, "For some writers, style not only reveals the spirit of the man, it reveals his identity, as surely as would his fingerprints."

When you begin to pay attention, you can spot the differences in style between magazines or newspapers or how one writer uses the language as compared to another. The subtle differences are so distinctive that there are now computer programs that can analyze pieces of writing, looking at which words are used and how they're put together, and more often than not identifying the author with uncanny accuracy.

Let's take a really easy example. The major New York newspapers are pretty well split between the tabloids—the *New York Post* and the *New York Daily News*—and that "great gray lady," *The New York Times*. If the *Post* and *Daily News* talk like teens in the hood, their sober-sided sister more resembles a Victorian grandmother with a poker up her spine.

Take the opening paragraph covering the same event in December 2004:

* *New York Daily News*: "A gutsy narcotics detective who followed a pistol-packing thug into a seedy

Bronx building alone suffered two bullet wounds during a fierce struggle yesterday—but still managed to shoot the teenage gunman dead, police said."

* *The New York Times*: "A gunfight in an apartment building in the Bronx yesterday left a man dead and the detective who shot him to death wounded, the police said."

Both stories give you the facts, but their styles are 180 degrees apart. The *Daily News* is a tabloid paper, and it aims to involve its readers. To do this it employs almost a fiction technique and slathers on the adjectives and adverbs. *The New York Times*, long one of journalism's icons, announces on its masthead that it publishes "All the news that's fit to print." The paper opts for "just the facts." Which style is better? That's the stuff of endless debates. Which do you prefer? That's the stuff of style—and what sells newspapers.

In these cases, style has to do with appropriateness. In a tabloid newspaper, the informal style of the *Daily News* is acceptable. If the same story style appeared in one of the national newsmagazines or on a PBS report, undoubtedly it would be received with a raised eyebrow.

However, *The New York Times* isn't without its own purple prose moments. Read a restaurant review, and you'll see tabloid-style prose overlaid with "gray lady" sophistication. Catch this description of a Japanese chicken dish: "a shockingly succulent deboned young chicken luxuriated under a light soy glaze and a dusting of sansho pepper." Yeah, right. Whatever.

What we're going to do in this chapter is show you what's appropriate in various writing situations, as well as explain how you can identify your own style and amalgamate it into your communications.

Write the Way You Talk

This is perhaps the most difficult ability to master if it doesn't come naturally. Think of Garrison Keillor on National Public Radio. When you read his books, they sound just like he does when he's on the radio. You feel a bond with the man because he's right there on the page in front of you. Too often we're trying so hard to be grammatically correct and to say "meaningful things" that we forget to be ourselves.

When you try too hard, it's like putting on a three-piece suit, a starched shirt, and a tasteful tie, thinking you'll have as much fun as if you were in sweats and running shoes. Of course, this is not the case. Your whole attitude will be changed because you'll feel confined. You have to live up to your look. It's better to aim for "sweats-style" writing.

One suggestion for those who become terrified at the thought of putting words on paper is to go to a park or to your most comfortable place in the house, flip on a tape recorder, and talk through what you want to convey. No one's going to hear it but you, so don't get hung up on pronunciation, grammar, or voice quality. Often people who are afraid of writing find they can talk a blue streak. When you're talked out, sit down at the word processor and listen to what you want to say. If you're a good typist, transcribe it word for word, but you'll find there will be changes, so you're probably fine just jotting down ideas.

Heads Up ✳

Forget the business suit mentality. Today, except in the most formal writing, verbs are contracted and not every sentence follows the guidelines you were handed in school. It's OK to be conversational as long as your tone matches your audience.

You're going to be more conservative when writing for your church bulletin than for your high school reunion program. If you're turning out a report for your boss, you'll want to be direct and serious. When you're toasting your brother the night before his wedding, you'll be able to show the irreverent humor that's more the real you.

K.I.S.S. (Keep It Simple, Seriously)

Ernest Hemingway, a master of style, said, "My aim is to put down on paper what I see and what I feel in the best and simplest way." The true secret to good writing is to keep it simple. Cut out the superfluous adjectives and adverbs. Let the nouns and verbs shout your message without adornment.

In the seventeenth century, naturalist John Ray said, "He that uses many words for explaining any subject, doth, like the cuttlefish, hide himself for the most part in his own ink." That's the hard part. Cutting down the piles of purple prose into a lean, trim series of sentences that get your point across without requiring your reader to use a road map.

The shorter the piece you're writing, the more difficult it's going to be to stay simple and succinct. Mark Twain summed it up when he said, "I didn't have time to write a short letter, so I wrote a long one instead." If you have to write a twenty-five-word newspaper ad or a one-page report, allow yourself at least twice as much time as you would if the piece were going to be twice as long. Our rule is: Shorter takes longer.

Here's a process that we both highly recommend:

1. Begin by dumping everything you can think of into an electronic file or onto a piece of paper. Don't worry about grammar, syntax, or style. Just write down the ideas you want to get across.
2. Next, go over it and highlight the parts that are really important, what must stay and what can be junked. Rewrite—or cut and paste—so only the important parts remain.
3. Now, shape the new piece, trimming words, finding stronger, more compelling verbs. Take out words as if they were part of a Pick-Up-Sticks pile. By that we mean carefully, so you don't upset the order of those words left on the page.
4. Once you've gotten the piece exactly the way you want it—and before declaring the job done—go away from it for a time. Do something else. Clear your brain. Then come back and read it aloud. You may find other places that need to be tweaked—or you may be ready to do Snoopy's dance on top of the doghouse because it's perfect.

The point is, simple is best and short takes longest. Simple and short are both worth the time and trouble.

K.D.'s Proofreading Perspective ✹

In an earlier tip, I recommended that you *always* ask some-one else to proofread your work before submitting it, and I stand by that 1,000 percent. But a caution for those times when you're tempted to show people your work and ask for comments. Everyone has a different perspective, and if you show it to five different people, you're likely to get five different opinions and ten or more suggestions on what would be great to add, delete, or change. Outside opinions can be valuable, but follow your instincts on what you think is right for you. That's not a bad way to approach life, either, to my way of thinking.

Clichés—We're Not Kidding

The Plain English Campaign is a British independent pressure group that's lobbying for public information to be written in understandable English. As of early 2005 the organization claimed to have eight thousand registered supporters in eighty countries.

In March 2004 the campaign issued a press release reporting the results of a poll among members as to the most irritating phrases in the language. The cliché voted most overused was "at the end of the day." Next came "at this moment in time."

We're happy to give you some of the clichés we see all the time and delete just as often.

address the issue
awesome
basically
between a rock and
  a hard place
bottom line
challenge (instead of
  problem)
glass half full
  (or half empty)
going forward
I hear what you're saying
in terms of . . .
it's not rocket science
let me share with you
literally

on the same page	think outside the box
piece of cake	to be perfectly honest
pushing the	touch base
envelope	value-added

We bet you can think of dozens more expressions you don't want to hear again, even though you know you will. In 1946 English writer George Orwell said, "Never use a metaphor, simile, or other figure of speech that you are used to seeing in print." Today he would have also warned against those you hear on radio, on television, and in films. Does anyone need to hear "Show me the money!" or "Make my day!" or "yada, yada, yada" again? We didn't think so. Those memorable lines were great fun the first few weeks, but give it a rest!

It's easy to fall into the common vernacular. Rather than thinking up new ways of expressing yourself, it's simpler to rely on old trite-but-true phrases. If you want to have your listeners and readers tune in to what you're saying, find new ways of phrasing your ideas. If you get discouraged, remember the words of American author Nathaniel Hawthorne: "Easy reading is damned hard writing."

Getting Down to Business

Business writing is a necessity for most of us. You may not have to write reports, but at some point you're almost certainly going to be writing a letter or a memo or a notice for the bulletin board. There are basic guidelines you can use to make your business communications more powerful.

Be Clear

One rule that always holds when writing any kind of discussion paper, be it a school essay or college term paper or business report, is

> Say what you're going to say (opening).
> Say it (body).
> Say what you said (close).

It's just that uncomplicated. In the opening paragraph, describe the topic you're going to be discussing. In the body of the paper, discuss it. In the final paragraph, summarize your conclusions or restate your thesis and proof. Follow that outline, and it will be almost impossible for you or your reader to get lost.

To achieve this clarity, you need to think and write with purpose. Consider the results you're looking for before you begin to sling words at the paper—or, more likely, into a computer file. You might want to ask yourself the following questions before you begin any project:

* What do I want done?
* Have I clearly thought out the result I want from this communication?
* Is there a clearly stated time frame?
* Who needs to be involved (not just departments but actual names)?
* Do I need to give any special instructions?
* What could go wrong, and how can the company circumvent the problem?

If you have those answers identified before you start to put bytes in the file, we guarantee that your words will flow more easily and your ideas will be clearly expressed.

Another clarity issue centers around the words you use. We talked about this in Chapter 7 when we examined vocabulary, and we'll explore the issue again in Chapter 10 when we look at the regional and generational differences in the language. Too often we forget that although we know our industry jargon or our local slang, our audience may not be on the same wavelength. You have to do your homework and understand your audience before you choose the words you'll use. If you're an engineer writing for other engineers, you're pretty safe using the industry vernacular. If you're an engineer writing for the rest of us, stick to words we'll understand—or lead us through the definitions so we know what you're talking about.

Which brings us to what words *denote* versus what they *connote*. Don't panic. Those are $20 words for 50¢ ideas. What a word denotes is the dictionary definition, its exact or explicit meaning. What a word connotes is the feeling or mood that people associate with it. The classic example is probably describing someone as a *nice* guy. Do you mean he's really a pleasant person who's fun to be around, or do you mean he's so dull there's nothing else to say about him?

Another classic example is that an *assertive man* is a leader, whereas an *assertive woman* is a witch. If you hear that the new department head is *frugal*, do you think "careful with money" or a "cheap penny-pincher"? How you react to a word is based on your background, your experiences, your personal history. When you write *car*, your readers are probably going to think of the car they're driving, which means that some will think sedan, others will go to SUV, others to a sports car. If you really meant a hatchback, none of your readers may be tuned in to that wavelength. Be very specific in what you say. Think about the different connotations of the words you use. Your audience will thank you for it.

Be Concise

Know what you're trying to say, and then say it as clearly and concisely as possible. You don't need lots of words to make your point. In fact, if you get too wordy, the reader may wonder what you're trying to cover up. The British prime minister Winston Churchill, a prolific author and speaker, said, "Say what you have to say, and the first time you come to a sentence with a grammatical ending—sit down." That's good advice if not taken so literally that the first time you plant a period at the end of a sentence you quit. You won't get away with cutting things short that easily.

Another consideration is that when you ramble on and on, your reader may have no idea what you're talking about. In 1998 the *San Jose Mercury News* reported that a business magazine had asked readers to submit idiotic quotes from their managers. Our favorite was reportedly the final paragraph in a national press release from a major Silicon Valley technology firm. It said, "[The company] is endeavorily determined to promote constant attention on current procedures of transacting business focusing emphasis on innovative ways to better, if not supersede, the expectations of quality!" Say what? How much better to write that the company "pays strict attention to improving business transactions and emphasizing innovation as a way to surpass quality expectations." Or better yet, "We're trying every day to improve and surpass our already high quality service." As we said earlier, K.I.S.S. (Keep It Simple, Seriously).

Lose the Little Words

In a valiant but misguided attempt to clarify our meaning, we often muddy the waters even more.

It is an easy way to get out of our pattern of bad habits and to do something that we might find is more productive in the long run.

Whew! That sounds like something we wrote when a teacher was counting the words and we were coming up short. Let's take that down a peg or two by eliminating all the unnecessary little words that don't add anything to the meaning.

~~It is an easy way to~~ get out of ~~our pattern of~~ bad habits ~~and to~~ do something ~~that we might find is more~~ productive ~~in the long run~~.

OK, now we add a more powerful verb (*eliminate* instead of *get out of*) and rewrite the sentence.

We can eliminate our bad habits by doing something productive.

Aha! Clean, simple, and easy to understand. It doesn't get better than that.

Setting Up a Style Sheet

K.D., along with every other proofreader and editor worth their salt, will tell you that a style sheet is one of the most important documents in your file. There are all sorts of resources to tell you how certain spelling, punctuation, capitalization, and reference issues are generally handled in publishing and the media. That's fine and dandy, but you need to know how your particular business or client handles them. In your office, is it *email* or *e-mail*? Is *Internet* capitalized? How about *website*? One word or two? Capital *W* or small?

Does your product require a trademark (™) or a registered (®) symbol when it's mentioned for the first time? Current editions of *The Associated Press Stylebook* and *The Chicago Manual of Style* are the most commonly used sourcebooks; however, they'll be superseded by your organization's style sheet.

K.D.'s Proofreading Perspective

I've probably created close to one hundred style sheets in the last twenty years, and depending on what the client wanted, they've ranged from less than a page to more than two hundred pages. When I'm boiling down for clients what they might want to consider for a style sheet, I suggest two "areas":

* Items that could be handled more than one way, specifying the company's choice (as in the *email* versus *e-mail* and *Website* versus *website* examples).

* Those items that you don't want the other people working on your documents (writers, editors, proofreaders, designers, clients) to repeatedly have to look up (as in trademarked product names). Or even common words that come up so often that it's hard to remember how they should be handled, such as *clear-cut* and *reenter*. (Yup, you're seeing that correctly: *reenter* should not be hyphenated as *re-enter*.)

If your company or client doesn't have a style sheet, you can make yourself a hero or heroine by establishing one. It doesn't have to be very complicated. Basically, what you're doing is writing down how the company or client wants certain terms used, any particular spellings, etc.

Style sheets can be organized in a number of different ways, but the primary categories are usually the following:

* **Conventions.** For example,

   Use a series comma: red, green, and blue.

   Italicize important words in text: *consistency* is the key.

* **Numbers.** For example,

   Spell out one to nine, and use numerals for 10 and above.

   Phone numbers/area codes: (415) 555-0914

* **Words and terms.** For example,

   coauthor
   e-mail
   spell-checker

   Here is a portion of a sample house style sheet:

Pacific Advertising Agency
accents: not with capital letters
   (café au lait, but CAFE AU LAIT)
don't use series commas
comic strip and radio program titles:
   in quotes

magazine and record album titles: ital
airdate
a.m.
catalog
disc (compact disc, disc jockey)
disk (computer disk)
Northern California
point-of-sale advertising (POS)
PR firm
SASE (an SASE)

As you can see, what the style sheet does is give you a way to be consistent throughout all written correspondence.

Toni's Tidbits 🍁

Consistency is one of K.D.'s favorite words and one of my least favorite. (Note from K.D.: Yes, for me it's a way of life, and I drive many people crazy trying to ensure it—but my clients love me for it!) She will point out that I used a word three ways in one paragraph: hyphenated, not hyphenated, and capitalized. It's not easy being me. My blithe disregard for the conventions of spelling and hyphenation isn't my best quality. I admit it. And I'm not a good proofreader. I just don't notice the little glitches that K.D. sees as glaring errors.

However, I do admit she's correct. Consistency is the hallmark of a good letter or memo or report or any other communication. When I don't have K.D. to sweep up after me, I am much more cautious about whether or not everything matches as it should.

We're insistent: be consistent. (OK, K.D., are you happy now?) (Yes I am. Thank you, Toni.)

Even if you have a corporate style sheet, here are eight areas that may not be covered but that often cause problems or confusion, along with some guidelines on how to handle them like a pro:

1. One common rule for numbers is to spell out one through nine but to use numerals for 10 and above unless the company has a different style. Don't start or end a sentence with a numeral—spell it out instead.

Twenty-one cheerleaders kept the crowd enthused.

The "crowd" at the reading was a measly seven.

2. In titles, capitalize the first word and every important word. Unimportant words are articles, conjunctions, and prepositions (although prepositions five letters and longer are often capitalized—e.g., Underneath, Above).

3. Capitalize titles if they precede a name:

Emphatically and without hesitation, President Harrington and former president Hill denied any wrongdoing.

John Harrington, the president of Upsy-Daisy Trampolines, jumped bail.

4. For company names, follow the capitalization the company uses, e.g., Woods and Streams Investment Company, Inc.

5. Capitalize all proper nouns, e.g., Denmark, Tivoli Gardens, the Little Mermaid, Hamlet.

6. Accepted practice dictates that you use the full name of someone at first mention and then last name only.

> Otis P. Snerdly in accounting questioned the report. Snerdly said, "Something doesn't add up."

(Some newspapers require Mr., Ms., Dr., etc., with every mention of a last name. Check to see how your company or client wants names handled.)

7. Avoid negative constructions. They set a bad tone and often make confusing sentences.

> There's no way *Survivor* contestants could miss the shark circling offshore. (negative)

> The *Survivor* contestants clearly saw the shark circling offshore. (positive)

Another tip for avoiding negative construction is to look at any sentence in which you've used the word *but* to see if *and* could be substituted. *But* is a negation or modification of whatever was said before it.

> The Thanksgiving Day parade was the biggest ever, but Santa showed up last. (negative)

> The Thanksgiving Day parade was the biggest ever, and Santa showed up last. (positive light on negative situation)

Notice how people speak, and you'll see a trend toward negative construction.

> "Is it going to rain today?"

"I don't think so." (How about, "It's supposed to be sunny"?)

"Thank you."

"No problem." (How about, "You're welcome"?)

Listen to yourself and look at your writing to see if you're falling into the negative trap.

8. Use parallel construction to make your writing clearer to the reader. Parallelism means that expressions with similar content should be similar in construction. Here are some examples of parallelism:

> **"Ask not what your country can do for you. Ask what you can do for your country."**

> **". . .** government **of the people, by the people, for the people . . ."**

> The promotion went to the person who **worked** hard, **showed** promise, and **played** politics.

The point is that you don't want to switch horses in midstream. If Lincoln had said, "government of the people, who would also run it for the common good," we bet no one would remember the Gettysburg Address. That's the power of parallel construction.

A Final Word

It seems as if there are a lot of things to remember, and we hope your eyes aren't glazing over. Mastering English isn't as difficult as it sometimes sounds. We work with words every day, and still we look up usage rules regularly. What you have to remember is that writing isn't easy for anyone. Some people who write a lot make it look, to the casual observer, simpler than it is. When you get frustrated because you don't think of yourself as a writer, reflect on the wise words of Nobel Prize–winning novelist Thomas Mann: "A writer is a person for whom writing is more difficult than it is for other people."

Fifteen Tips for Better Writing

Instead of pulling tips from the chapter, we're giving you fifteen new ways you can make your writing cleaner and more compelling:

1. **Be brief.** Keep content and titles as short as possible to catch and hold your reader's attention. Where feasible, replace paragraphs with bulleted lists.
2. **Be specific.** Get right to the point and say what you mean, cutting out all the fluff. Concentrate on the message you want to get across.
3. **Be accurate.** Double-check your spelling, punctuation, capitalization, and facts. Read the piece aloud to catch more errors, and, if you can, let someone else check it, too.
4. **Make your parts of speech agree.** Be sure the pronouns correctly reflect the nouns they're replacing and the verbs agree with their subjects.
5. **Use nouns instead of pronouns as sentence subjects.** Pronouns can cause confusion about who or what they refer to. Use nouns whenever possible to avoid ambiguity.
6. **Be consistent.** Use the same style of wording and formatting for all similar elements, such as titles, headings, lists, and numbers.

7. **Use simple sentences.** Keep your message strong by keeping your sentences short. Instead of connecting thoughts with *and* or *whereas*, use a period. Start a new sentence for the new thought.

8. **Put important content first.** Lead with your core conclusion, and then describe how you reached it.

9. **Stick to a single topic.** Try to discuss only one topic in each article, memo, e-mail, or letter. When your point stands alone, it will stand out.

10. **Know and target your audience.** Use only vocabulary your audience will understand. Define any terms you think will confuse them.

11. **Include a call to action.** If you're looking for a specific result, ask for it. If your readers don't know exactly what they are expected to do, they won't do anything. "Every time you make a phone call, write it down in a phone log."

12. **Use *you* instead of the third person.** Involve your readers by speaking to them directly, instead of using the impersonal *he, she,* or *they.*

13. **Use the active voice, not the passive.** Focus on who's doing it, not on what's being done. "The children struck the piñata," not "The piñata was struck by the children."

14. **Be respectful.** Be politically correct, no matter how you personally feel. Be alert to racial, ethnic, religious, or gender bias in everything you say.

15. **Be positive, not negative.** Talk about what your audience should do, not what they shouldn't do. "Do it right" gives a much more powerful message than "Don't mess up."

INTERNET ENGLISH

Be Trilingual in One Language

ONCE UPON A TIME, if you could speak English so you were understood, you were considered a step ahead of the pack. Later, if you could also write English, you were installed behind the big desk at the front of the local one-room schoolhouse. Today, it's a little more complicated than that. You have to know which version of English to use in what situation, whether you're being heard, being read, or interacting on the Internet—it's three languages in one. In this chapter we're going to discuss the different ways English is used on the Internet, when you're speaking to a global audience, and in e-mail, when you hope you're not.

English on the Internet

In the mid-1990s, the Internet was just coming of age, moving away from being a techie tool and becoming an essential educational, business, and communication avenue not only for Americans but for the rest of the world. We were suddenly global. What was typed in Topeka was read in Taipei in the blink of an eye. You could get from New Delhi to New York in a heartbeat. Sandusky was suddenly a neighbor of Singapore.

When we first got involved with websites, we found we had a new language to learn because the Internet doesn't work quite like other communication media. E-mails were casual conversation, somewhere between a letter and a phone call. However, without voice inflection or opportunity to judge the receiver's reaction, words could be misinterpreted. Meanings could be shifted. The ease of forwarding messages—along with the ability to respond to everyone instead of just the sender—means private communications could become public. Ouch!

Furthermore, we had to design ways to convey large amounts of information to people who weren't accustomed to reading or learning on a computer screen. We couldn't rely on sophisticated graphics because they couldn't be read by often unsophisticated corporate computers. Want to send your IT (Information Technology) department into orbit? Just try downloading an application they haven't approved. Amazingly, some of the largest companies were operating with the most outdated software. Instead of flash and dash graphic effects, we had to figure out how to make the material compelling for the most basic applications. We found the secrets to effective communication were simple language, logical sequences, and lots of white space. How does this relate to you? Try using simple language, logical sequences, and lots of white space on anything you write online, and we guarantee you'll find your recipients will be more receptive than if you don't.

Global English Translated

If you have an e-mail address, if you sell on eBay, if you have a website—in fact, if you have any Web presence at all—you can connect internationally with most of the world. While American English is widely spoken, it's not widely spoken well, even in America. On the Internet, many folks just hit the translate button, and your words are instantly morphed into their language. Just read the instructions that came with your VCR or another foreign-made appliance if you want to see how well strict translation works. We rest our case.

That means you must be very conscious of the information you convey, how you word your messages, and how you present yourself. Here are twelve guidelines that have served us well when working on the Internet, whether we're trying to reach next door or the next continent:

1. Keep sentences short. Grammatically complicated constructions may sound great, but they're difficult to translate, especially when a software program does the conversion. If you know another language you can see how meanings can get lost if the sentences aren't short and direct. Go to http://world.altavista.com and enter a sentence or two in English and let them translate it into another language you speak. You'll immediately see that simple is better. Overall, the Babel Fish software does a remarkable job, but if the material you entered is convoluted or slangy, the translation may be word-for-word but not necessarily accurate. It can't be without the nuances only a human can give it. Don't let your genius turn into gibberish. For the Internet, write as simply as possible using basic vocabulary and straightforward sentences.

2. Be aware of multiple meanings. We warned about slang usage in Chapter 7, and we need to warn again here. There are many terms we use that aren't common to British English and therefore wouldn't be understood by those who learned somewhere other than in the United States. Err on the side of caution. For instance, instead of saying, "We used to go," say, "We often went." We understand *used to* as an auxiliary verb, but many non-American speakers don't. Instead of saying, "It is hard," say, "It is difficult." *Hard* wouldn't be readily understood as a synonym for *difficult*. In the following list, we give you some typical American idioms and their more acceptable global English translations. The list, developed by K.D. and her associate Merilee Eggleston, is a great reminder of how often we turn to slang to get our points across—and thereby sometimes fail miserably.

Idiom to Avoid	Suggested Substitution
800 number	toll-free number
boot camp	course, class
bottom line	final result
bread and butter	primary revenue source
burnout	exhaustion
come up to speed	learn
connect the dots	put together, assemble
cutting edge	innovative, new
deal (noun)	transaction
deal with	manage

draw on	rely on
drill down	analyze, research
flag (verb)	mark, highlight
free lunch	benefit, for free
from scratch, or from the ground up	from the beginning
geared toward	designed for, intended for
golden rule	primary principle
holy grail	ultimate reward, ultimate goal
housekeeping	general administration
jump to conclusions	assume
keep an eye out	watch for
left in the dust	outpaced
lion's share	majority
living hand to mouth	a marginal existence
make the grade	pass
only game in town	sole opportunity
on the fly	in real time, hastily, spontaneously
out of the question	impossible
pay off	be worth the effort
plus much more	and much more
raise the bar	increase expectations
ready for prime time	prepared for
road warrior	mobile worker, salesperson
rule of thumb	general principle
sliding scale	range
think outside the box	think creatively
toe the line	adhere to the rule
turnkey	complete, easily deployed
up and running	operating
with an eye toward	focus, goal

3. Include all articles and verbs. We save time and space—not to mention wear and tear on our manicures—by writing in an abbreviated style called *telegraphic*, omitting articles and verbs. We mentioned earlier that newscasters do this on radio and television. On the Internet, it's even more prevalent.

> All invited to the conference-over bash. (Huh?)

> Everyone is invited to the party after the conference. (Got it!)

When writing for a global audience, flesh out the sentence and skip the cute turns of phrase.

4. Keep *that* in the sentence. We've been taught to drop *that* when writing for clarity and style, even though we say it constantly in spoken English because it adds rhythm to our words—and sometimes provides that extra split-second we need to marshal our thoughts. An audio script will be riddled with *that*s, while a formal paper might include very few.

Global English speakers can be confused if *that* is missing. Your sentences will be longer but clearer if you remember to include *that* wherever it makes sense.

> Here is an idea under consideration. (Huh?)

> Here is an idea **that is** under consideration. (Got it!)

5. Limit acronyms. Acronyms stay the same no matter how they're translated, but often the words aren't the same in another language, so the acronym makes no sense to the foreign reader. Companies like IBM or GM have turned the acronym into their corporate logo and it will hold globally, but neither ASAP (As Soon As Possible) nor PDQ (Pretty Darn Quick) will get anyone offshore moving faster.

6. Avoid humor. Ask any comedian—what plays in Pittsburgh won't play in Peoria, so how could you expect a joke from Chicago to rock the rafters in Nairobi? It isn't going to happen. Save your humor for people you know, those who are as familiar with the language and the culture as you are.

7. Watch for U.S.-centric wording. When writing for a global audience, be careful that your perspective doesn't unwittingly offend your reader. When we talk about things that are *foreign* or *alien* or from *third-world countries*, we may not mean to show bias, but it can be interpreted that way.

You also need to be specific. If writing about the government or the president or the flag, make sure you say the U.S. government, the U.S. president, or the U.S. flag. Other countries have governments, presidents, and flags, too—although they don't think we know that. Let's be careful to show that we're clued in.

8. Include state and country with city names. We know that Dallas is in Texas, but we can't expect a global audience to have a comprehensive recollection of our fifty states and their major cities. Americans have enough trouble just remembering the countries on each continent, let alone all the internal states or provinces within each country. Always indicate a city's state and/or country. Are you talking about Marseilles, Illinois, or Marseilles, France? For that matter, do you mean Kansas City, Kansas, or Kansas City, Missouri? You can't be too specific.

9. Specify time by date, not season. When it's spring-time in Paris, it's autumn in Australia, so talking about a new campaign that will launch in the spring isn't going to excite everyone in the same way. Indicate time by date, month, or quarter, not by season.

> The new campaign is scheduled for a second quarter launch.

Heads Up 🖋

It's safest to spell out dates instead of using our American system of indicating month, day, and year. The rest of the world reverses the month and day. If you want something done by 10/08/05, it could be interpreted as August 10 in countries that would write that date 8/10/05. If you mean October 8, write it out.

10. Avoid apostrophes, exclamation points, and ampersands. Not all punctuation and abbreviations translate to other languages, so some readers might not recognize them. To make sure you're understood, spell out words instead of using contractions (*it is* instead of *it's*, *we will* instead of *we'll*, *you are* instead of *you're*). Avoid the possessive apostrophe, too. Say, "the speed of the printer" rather than "the printer's speed." In the same fashion, avoid using exclamation points and ampersands (&). They will only confuse some in your audience.

11. Avoid slashes. Part of our written "shorthand" in American English is to put a slash between two words in place of *and* or *or*.

We're looking for **a man/woman** who can mend our fences. (Huh?)

To avoid confusion, spell out what the slash is meant to indicate.

We're looking for **either a man or a woman** who can mend our fences. (Got it!)

12. Be careful with graphics. There are numerous American symbols—the red octagon (stop), the hand with a thumb raised (thumbs up), the thumb and first finger against the forehead (loser), the check mark (√) for OK, etc.—that either may not be understood or may be insulting in other cultures. To be safe, except for the international forbid sign (a circle enclosing a picture with a red slash through it), stay away from symbols.

Another issue with graphics is that what we consider commonplace, other cultures may find offensive or obscene. While miniskirts, hands, soles of feet, alcoholic beverages, and such are perfectly acceptable in our culture, they are red flags elsewhere. Don't risk a relationship because of a mindless graphic.

If you follow these suggestions for writing global English on the Internet—and for that matter, in any newsletters, brochures, or other promotional material that may have global distribution—you'll find easier acceptance by new friends in other places.

E-Mail—It's Just a Letter

One thing to be very sure about, e-mail isn't *just* anything. It's becoming as standard as the telephone and more used than "snail mail." We forget that every e-mail message is, in effect, being etched into stone because someone, somewhere, sometime, somehow will be able to resurrect it. Few things are as inaccurately named as the *delete key* on a computer. You can delete all you want, but others can still retrieve. Ask Microsoft or Martha Stewart about the indestructibility of e-mail. Both of them had the prosecution produce e-mails as evidence against them in court. (If Bill Gates can't destroy an e-mail, what chance do we have?)

So what you write can come back and bite you. That's the first thing to keep in mind when you send a scathing note to a coworker calling your boss a pusillanimous nincompoop. If the boss finds out what that means (cowardly idiot), you're going to be in trouble. Experience has proven if you say something negative, it will wind up on his or her desktop. Guaranteed.

Here are some tips to keep in mind the next time you sit down to dash off a diatribe to thirty or forty of your nearest and dearest friends:

* **Be brief.** E-mails should be informational without being encyclopedic. Spare us the message from an acquaintance that requires scrolling for pages. Put the additional information, if you must, in an attachment. Just because there's no extra postage, don't feel you can blather on endlessly. Get to the point.

Obviously, when you're writing to close friends or family, that rule doesn't necessarily apply. Lots of families use e-mails like round-robin letters, passing them from one household to another with everyone adding their two cents for the benefit of the clan. They're great fun to get and send. However, if you're writing to acquaintances or in business situations, brief is better.

❋ **Curb your enthusiasm.** Have you ever gotten an e-mail so filled with !!!!!s and ;-)s and SHOUTING CAPITALS, along with other pop-up or scroll-down gimmicks that you wanted to scream? Of course, we all have. There's something about an e-mail that brings out the rah-rah cheerleader. Some of the *emoticons*, those silly faces created from punctuation marks, are cute, and, if used with a modicum of restraint, they can make a point or indicate an emotion. If they are sprinkled like confetti at a ticker tape parade, they are annoying—and demonstrate a certain lack of vocabulary. Let your words carry your excitement. They'll do just fine if you let them.

❋ **Check for errors before you send.** In 2003 Microsoft released the results of a consumer survey about e-mail mistakes. The top mistake (41 percent) was forgetting to include an attachment. The next two were misspellings (34 percent) and sending the e-mail before it was ready (32 percent). Those are two that can be easily corrected.

Some e-mail programs have a built-in spell-check component, but you know what we think of those. Another solution is to have a dictionary at hand so you can double-check any spelling that looks suspicious. Easier yet, write the message in a Word or other program file, notice what is flagged as wrong, correct it, and only then copy and paste the message into your e-mail. Treat your e-mails with the same care you would give your handwritten correspondence. Your signature may not be in ink on an e-mail, but it's just as representative of you.

Heads Up

This has nothing to do with grammar, but it's a great tip if you are concerned about sending an e-mail before it's ready. Put the address in last, when everything else is written, corrected, and ready. The e-mail can't go anywhere if there's nowhere to go.

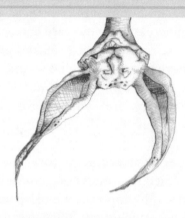

Twelve Tips to Be Trilingual at Home and Abroad

Obviously, the Internet has changed the way we live, research, and interact. It's also changing the way we handle the language. Here are some reminders that will help you become a webmaster:

1. Simple language, logical sequences, and lots of white space are some of the secrets of effective online communication, both locally and globally.
2. Say things as simply as possible using basic vocabulary and straightforward sentences.

3. The rule of thumb if you're going to make the grade is to write without slang so your message pays off.

4. Include all the articles and verbs—and even *that*—in your sentences for clarity.

5. Acronyms and humor usually don't translate.

6. Be sensitive to your reader by avoiding U.S.-centric terms and by spelling out the state (or country) where a city is located.

7. Spell out dates and times instead of using numbers.

8. Avoid apostrophes, exclamation points, ampersands, *and* or *or* slashes, and graphics that won't be understood or could be misinterpreted.

9. Think carefully before you write an e-mail that expresses strong emotions.

10. The strongest e-mail messages are brief and to the point.

11. Let your words, not symbols, convey your enthusiasm and your respect for other people's sensibilities.

12. Proofread every e-mail before you send it because your errors will say more about you than your message will.

REGIONALSPEAK

Our Common Language Isn't the Same

IT ALL BOILS DOWN to this. The most important reason for any language's existence is to communicate one person's thoughts to another person. It sounds simple, but there's a hitch. The person you're talking to has to understand you, and, even if you're both speaking English, there's no guarantee your vocabularies match. Let's look at what affects the way we speak. Who we are and where we live and how long we've been on the planet—and a bunch of other influences—all affect our language, for better or for worse. We don't want you to change a lot, just to be aware of how we all differ. As they say in New Orleans' French Quarter, "Vive la difference!"

More than ever before, today we are divided by the barrier of a common language. What we say, how we say it, and what things are called differ from one part of the country to another and sometimes from one part of a state to another. We'll introduce you to some of these regional quirks and tell you how to handle them with aplomb.

Just a Little Background

We live in a world with transparent borders. Whatever happens anywhere in our country or around the world, there is always someone with a camera, a microphone, or a cell phone available to send back a report to the hungry media.

There was a time in the United States when the news came out of New York and the newscasters had Eastern seaboard accents and were carefully taught at NBC's training school for announcers and at those select colleges and universities that included courses designed for the next generation of broadcasters. By the mid-1960s, the charm of regional accents had started to creep in. Announcers no longer sounded pompous and self-absorbed, usually standing with one hand cupped to their ear to better hear their ringing tones. Listeners preferred the folksy sound, the Arthur Godfrey down-home approach. Radio hosts were hired for their ability to entertain rather than for their enunciation. Formality began to break down. Instead of having news delivered from on high, we got it from someone who sounded like our neighbor chatting over the back fence. Newscasters became human beings, even capable of an emotion or two when the situation demanded it.

It was during the by-the-seat-of-our-pants reporting of President Kennedy's assassination that a newsman was seen in shirtsleeves, arguably for the first time—and he apologized for it. This was a brave new world in its infancy. Old rigid rules were being replaced, and societal barriers were coming down.

The result, or so you'd think, was that we would all speak the same language because everyone in the United States was privy to broadcasts by native speakers from every region of the country. From this should have come an amalgamated English that incorporated our hometown differences and evened out into a language Americans could all share equally. Wrong! All that happened was the standards lessened to the point that incorrect usage became the norm, and the rest of the world watched in bemused wonder as we began to lose our own language.

Many countries are like Italy. Natives speak their local dialect, but they also learn the national language. There was a time when if a Roman spoke to Toni in Italian, she could understand him perfectly. If he spoke his particular regional dialect, she was as lost as if he were speaking Sanskrit. In the United States, we don't worry about such language nuances. We speak the way the people around us speak, and if you don't understand, too bad.

Regional Oddities

While the media are busy trying to turn us into one unified nation, we still maintain our regional idiosyncrasies, heightened by the nomadic nature of Americans. By the time we hit retirement age, it's not uncommon to have lived in several diverse sections of the country, all the while assimilating those regionalisms into our speech.

Get in your car and drive around the country. You'll spot the differences. In Delaware, a *turnpike* refers to any highway, but in Florida, a *turnpike* is a toll road and an *inter-*

state is free. In the Midwest, if you're not on a *toll road*, you're on an *expressway* or a *highway*. In California, they look at you strangely if you don't use the *freeway*, while in many parts along the East Coast, you travel on a more genteel *parkway*.

You wear *sneakers* in New York but *tennis shoes* (or *tennies*) in Chicago. In an Indiana rainstorm, kids put on their *galoshes*, but in Boston, they wear their *rubbers*. This might account for the prophylactic being referred to as a *condom* on the East Coast instead of a *rubber* as it is in the Midwest.

In New York, you stand *on line*, not *in line* as we do other places, and if you *cut into line* in Wisconsin, it's called *budging*. In Chicago, you *go by* the show, rather than *going to* it, and even the show can be different. In the Midwest, you *see a show*, in other places you *go to the movies*, while in still others, you *catch a film*. Only the British and the occasional critic go to the *cinema*, but most big-city Americans watch films at the *cineplex*.

While most of us walk *side-by-side*, in Milwaukee, they walk *side-by-each*. In most places, we *go to the beach*, but in New Jersey, you *go down to the shore*. A *sidewalk* is called a *banquette* in New Orleans, but a *banquette* is a long upholstered bench against a wall to the rest of us. Most of us have *basements*, but in New Jersey, Philadelphia, and much of the rest of New England, they have *cellars*.

Social Differences

Because we move around so much, the language moves with us and the distinctions aren't as clear-cut. It was once easy to tell a person's social background by whether they referred to the *sofa*, the *divan*, or the *davenport*. Today, *couch* is pretty much heard everywhere, especially when the next word is *potato*.

Not so long ago, whether you said *vase* with a long *a* (*vayze*) or a short one (*vaahse*), whether you had *supper* with the family at six-thirty or with friends after the theater, and when you greeted guests in the foyer, whether you pronounced it *FOI-yeah* or *FOY-er* pretty much showed the world your level of acquaintance with country clubs and debutante balls. Today, a lot of those social differentials are disappearing, and we are playing it by ear, repeating the language we hear most often.

Heads Up ✹

Here's the key: wherever you are, speak so your audience understands and reacts the way you want.

Toni once asked a scientist at the Chicago Aquarium how to pronounce turbot (the fish). He said, "If I'm at a seminar discussing its environmental preferences, I say *TUR-bott*, but if I'm ordering it for dinner at a fancy French restaurant, I say *tur-BEAU*."

Take a lesson from that man! Tailor your language to your situation.

Generational Differences

Generational usage also changes the language. Your grandmother's *pocketbook* is your mother's *handbag* and your *purse*. Your *lapel pin* is your grandmother's *brooch*. She has an *icebox*, your mother has a *refrigerator*, and you have a *fridge*.

Your mother *heats in the oven*, you *nuke in the microwave*. Your grandfather *dials* an old friend, your father *calls up* a buddy, you *beep* him or *IM* (Instant Message) him or *give him a ring*.

When Toni's cousin had an operation many years ago, their grandmother whispered that Ann had had *female surgery*. Her mother reported grimly but quietly that she'd had a *tubal ligation*. Ann announced to the world that she'd had her *tubes tied*.

How we phrase things depends on how the words affect us. The older generations are more circumspect—well, the older generations we knew. When we get to that age, there will be much different issues on which we and "the kids" will disagree, but being circumspect about language probably won't be one of them. Who knows? We like to believe it's still a long way off.

Every generation has its own special way to use the language, its own list of proprieties and improprieties—although Generations X and Y seem to have very few things they won't talk about openly and without embarrassment. A sixteen-year-old daughter of friends waved on her way out the door, "I'm off like a prom dress." Not reassuring to her mother. When asked to explain, the teen said it was an everyday expression among her peers with no actual meaning except it sounded hip. The mother still worried.

The danger of being misunderstood falls more on the younger generation than the older. If you're speaking to someone in your grandmother's age group, tone it down. Keep things on a less blatant, more subtle footing. The same goes for people of obvious deep religious conviction. There are people who can be deeply offended by conversation you consider commonplace.

Heads Up

Think of the language you use as showing an element of respect as much as enhancing communication. If people don't understand what you're saying or are offended by it, your message won't get through. The trick is to think like the person you're talking to, get on their wavelength no matter how foreign it may sound to you. If you can't envision a word or phrase coming out of their mouths, don't let it come out of yours until they're out of earshot.

Pronunciation Can Be Everything

In *My Fair Lady*, Rex Harrison sang, "The French don't care what they do so much, as long as they pronounce it properly." That sure isn't the case in the United States. We have as many pronunciations as we have parts of the country. Then add in the various accents of nonnative speakers and you have a real hodge-podge.

So how are you supposed to know how a word is pronounced? Our best advice: ask!

Take city names. Natives of Louisville, Kentucky, say they live in *LOU-vul*. Chicagoans come from *cheek-AH-ga*, Detroiters hang out in *DEE-troit*, and in New Orleans, they'll tell you they live in *NOR-lins*.

Other geographical names follow much the same lack of rules. Houston (*HEW-ston*) is the city in Texas, while Houston (*HOW-ston*) is the street in New York. The Texas city of Elgin is pronounced with a hard g (*EL-ghin*), while

Elgin, Illinois, prefers a soft g (*EL-gin*). Peking (*Pee-KING*) is the city in China—or a great duck dish—while its namesake, Pekin (*PEEK-in*), Illinois, is a much less regal city. Milan (*Mill-AHN*) in Italy doesn't translate to the prison town of Milan (*MILE-un*) in Michigan. Bogota (*Ba-GO-da*), New Jersey, bears little relation to Bogotá (*Bo-go-TA*), Colombia. The challenge is to pick the correct place and pronunciation. The only people who can get it right are those who live there—and you can't always trust them.

In Chicago, Goethe Street is named after the German poet Johann Wolfgang von Goethe, so you might assume it would be pronounced *GRR-tuh*, as his name is. You'd be wrong. It's often pronounced *GO-thie* and sometimes *Go-EE-thee*. It's usually safest to have the cab driver drop you off at Scott, one street over.

It's amusing to listen to different reporters tell the same story. Iraq (*Ir-ACK* or *EYE-rack*) and each of its cities is given as many pronunciations as it has religious factions. Too often we hear Moscow pronounced as if it were a breed of dairy animal—there is no "cow" in Mosco(w). And there isn't a Michigan resident who doesn't cringe at least once or twice during the yearly yacht race when a network reporter talks about *Mackinack*. Mackinac Island is pronounced *Mackinaw*, just like the Windbreaker. We don't know why. It just is. Get with the program.

During one of Toni's previous incarnations, she was a classical music announcer. That's when she learned that proper names have no particular rules for pronunciation. The name bearer chooses how it is to be said. A definitive example is Hyacinth Bucket, the social-climbing lady of the house in the BBC television series *Keeping Up Appearances*. She insists to all comers that B-u-c-k-e-t is pronounced *boo-KAY*! And she's absolutely correct.

Do You Pronounce These Correctly?

Here are some other commonly mispronounced English words. Check them out. Are there any that give you trouble?

across—*a-CROSS*, **not** *a-CROST*
Arctic—*ARC-tic*, **not** *AR-tic*
asterisk—*AS-ter-isk*, **not** *AS-ter-ick*
athlete—*ATH-leet*, **not** *ATH-a-leet*
dilate—*DIE-late*, **not** *DIE-a-late*
electoral—*eh-LEK-tor-al*, **not** *eh-lek-TORY-al*
espresso—*ess-PRESS-oh*, **not** *ex-PRESS-oh*
February—*FEB-roo-ary*, **not** *FEB-you-ary*
federal—*FED-er-al*, **not** *FED-ral*
figure—*FIG-yer*, **not** *FIG-ger*
forte—*FORT*, **not** *for-TAY* (unless you're talking
   about loud music and then you say *FOR-tay*)
herb—*URB*, **not** *HURB* (the *h* is silent)
insouciant—*in-SOO-see-ant*, **not** *in-SOO-shant*
jewelry—*JOO-ell-ry*, **not** *JOOL-ry*
lambaste—*lam-BASTE*, **not** *lam-BAST*
library—*LIE-brer-ee*, **not** *LI-berry*
menstruation—*men-stroo-A-shun*, **not**
   men-STRAY-shun
mischievous—*MIS-chuh-vuhs*, **not** *miss-CHEEV-ious*
nuclear—*NOO-clee-ur*, **not** *NOO-ku-lur*
nuptial—*NUP-shul*, **not** *NUP-shoo-al*
often—*OFF-en*, **not** *OFT-en*
percolate—*PERC-o-late*, **not** *perc-U-late*
pianist—*PYAN-ist*, **not** *PEE-an-ist*
prescription—*PRE-scrip-tion*, **not** *PER-scrip-tion*
pronunciation—*pro-NUN-see-A-shun*, **not**
   pro-NOUN-see-A-shun

realtor—*REAL-tor*, **not** *REAL-A-tor*
respite—*RES-pit*, **not** *res-PITE*
sherbet—*SHER-bet*, **not** *SHER-BERT*
stereo—*STAIR-ee-oh*, **not** *STEER-ee-oh*
supremacist—*su-PREM-a-cist*, **not** *su-PREEM-ist*
triathlon—*tri-ATH-lon*, **not** *tri-ATH-a-lon*
verbiage—*VER-bi-age*, **not** *VER-bage*

Toni's Tidbits ✺

I'm back with another dreaded *however*. There are some words that are commonly mispronounced, but if you were to pronounce them correctly, you'd be in danger of being misunderstood. Two come to mind immediately.

Harass is supposed to be pronounced *HAIR-uss*, not *huh-RASS*, so you should talk about sexual *HAIR-uss-ment*, although dictionaries are bowing to popular usage and allowing *huh-RASS*. If that makes you *dour*, which most people pronounce *DOW-er*, like *sour*, but more correctly you'd be *DOER*, pronounced like *moor* or *poor*.

Time to repeat the language-is-for-communication mantra. Would you know what we were talking about if you heard the correct pronunciations? Most of us would have to stop for a moment and think about it.

I've long been an audio writer and producer, primarily for six- to sixteen-tape packages on business or self-development, the albums you buy from infomercials or at the back of the room after a seminar. My hard-and-fast rule remains that if a word wouldn't be understood when said correctly, we should go with the pronunciation in popular usage. In the list above, many of the mispronunciations are in popular usage and if you choose to use the correct pronunciation, you might be in the minority. It's your choice, but we want you to know what's correct, even if you decide not to use it. The last thing you want a listener to do is to stop and ask, "What did he say?" or "What is she talking about?"

I guarantee no one is going to rewind a tape or go back one track on a CD to listen again and figure it out. Just like vocabulary words—when in doubt, aim to be understood. Let the language snobs worry about being technically correct.

Five Rules to Being Understood By Your Audience

Here are five rules to remember when you're dealing with regional and pronunciation differences:

1. The most important reason for communication is to be understood; therefore, we have to try and recognize the differences in American English as it's spoken across the United States.
2. The rules for using language vary by generation, religious background, region, and common usage.
3. Don't pretend to speak the local slang unless you really know it as well as the natives, or you'll be spotted as a tourist in no time.
4. There are basic mistakes in pronunciation that can be remedied with a little study.
5. When choosing between correct and popular pronunciation, you may want to opt for the popular so you don't risk being misunderstood.

Appendix

Get It Right Every Time—Even When We're Not Here to Help

There are going to be times when you have questions and no answers. We've pulled together a list of our favorite go-to resources that you can access 24/7 to answer a question or double-check a grammar fact. Most are Internet sites, combined with a few classic books you should probably have in your library. To make it easier for you, we've listed the resources under the chapter they most relate to.

CHAPTER 1:

Good English—Whom Cares?

* Bartleby.com (bartleby.com). This is your dream library, online. From reference works to poetry to fiction to the classics, this site has the books—and the search tools. Look up facts, nail down quotations, or read a whole book, all right here.

* Do You Speak American? (pbs.org/speak/words). This part of the PBS website reflects the book *Do You Speak American?*, by Robert MacNeil and William Cran (Double-day, 2005). You'll find lists of words that shouldn't exist in anyone's vocabulary and be able to read essays and opinions on how Americans use English.

CHAPTERS 2 AND 3:
Covering the Basics: Parts of Speech, Punctuation Marks

* Acronym Finder (acronymfinder.com). Find definitions in seconds for more than 368,000 acronyms, abbreviations, and initialisms. A terrific tool, it lets you sort by category and industry.

* *The Elephants of Style*, by Bill Walsh (McGraw-Hill, 2004). Walsh, the copy chief of the *Washington Post*, has put together a witty but practical book that covers all areas of written English, including punctuation, grammar, and style.

* The Linguist List (linguistlist.org). Claiming to be the world's largest online linguistic resource, this serious site is staffed by linguistics professors and grad students. In its neat "Ask a Linguist" feature, sixty experts answer even your most perplexing grammar and punctuation questions.

* *The New Well-Tempered Sentence*, by Karen Elizabeth Gordon (Ticknor & Fields, 1993). The author gives you more information on punctuation than you probably want or need, but it's fun reading and will answer most questions.

CHAPTERS 4 AND 5:

Pronouns, Verbs

* Guide to Grammar & Writing (ccc.commnet.edu/grammar). This site will fill you in, good-naturedly, on anything you'd like to know about grammar and composition. It's nicely indexed and easy to use.

* Online Writing Lab (OWL) (http://owl.english.purdue.edu/writinglab). Purdue University has assembled an amazing site that gives you a wide assortment of grammar and writing tips, clearly stated and with lots of examples.

* *Woe Is I*, by Patricia T. O'Conner (Riverhead Hardcover, 2003). Easily referenced, this guide presents a wealth of practical information on a full range of grammar issues.

CHAPTER 6:

It's Only a Word

* *Bryson's Dictionary of Troublesome Words*, by Bill Bryson (Broadway Books, 2004). An entertaining writer takes on the good, the bad, and the ugly usages of words and phrases, organized in alphabetical order.

✳ Common Errors in English (wsu.edu/~brians/errors/index .html). Washington State University professor Paul Brians gives short answers to why certain usage is incorrect. His book *Common Errors in English Usage* (William, James Co., 2003) was taken from this popular site.

✳ *The Dictionary of Disagreeable English*, by Robert Hartwell Fiske (Writer's Digest Books, 2005). Dubbed "The Grumbling Grammarian," Fiske gives short, to-the-point advice on words and usage, arranged alphabetically for easy access.

✳ Thesaurus.com (http://thesaurus.reference.com). Have your way with words. This is your online lookup tool for synonyms and antonyms.

✳ *Word Court*, by Barbara Wallraff (Harcourt, 2000). The author, a senior editor at *The Atlantic Monthly*, has a commonsense attitude about language along with an eagle eye for what works and what doesn't.

CHAPTER 7:

Vivid Vocabulary and Superior Spelling

✳ Wordsmith (wordsmith.org). Anu Garg founded this site in 1994. Daily AWAD (A.Word.A.Day.) e-mails present a new word, its definition, and examples of current usage to more than 600,000 language lovers in two hundred countries. Garg supplements this with a weekly roundup of comments from readers around the world. An added bonus—the site archives all the defined words so you can catch any you may have missed.

✻ SpellCheck.net (http://spellcheck.net). Here's a spell-checker that really works. You can enter one word or a body of text up to twenty thousand characters. It also has math and language links that will handle almost any problem you encounter, whether it's making a conversion from teaspoons to tablespoons in the kitchen or translating into another language.

✻ Merriam-Webster Online (m-w.com). If you can't spell a word, how do you look it up? Answer: go to this site. All of *Merriam-Webster's Collegiate Dictionary* is here, plus search options that steer you to correct spellings and more. You can use the tenth edition for free, or subscribe to use the eleventh edition. And if you already own the eleventh—and we strongly suggest you do—a year's site subscription is free.

✻ Webopedia (webopedia.com). This is a great source for computer and Internet technology terms and definitions.

CHAPTER 8:

A Dose of Style

✻ *The Art of Styling Sentences*, by Ann Longknife, Ph.D., and K.D. Sullivan (Barron's, 2002). You'll find a witty, up-to-date review of the fundamentals of correct sentence structure, along with twenty basic sentence patterns that show you virtually every effective way of writing sentences.

✻ *The Associated Press Stylebook* (Basic Books, 2004). Arranged like a dictionary, the journalist's standard guide is available as a book or online (apstylebook.com) by subscription. With a site license, you can also customize it with your own entries. It's the easiest and most comprehensive "Am I writing it correctly?" guide for nonprofessionals.

✳ *The Chicago Manual of Style*, 15th ed. (University of Chicago Press, 2003). More for the professional editor, this standard style guide's website (chicagomanualofstyle.org/about.html) provides an online search tool that speeds you to answers in the print version.

✳ *The Elements of Style*, 4th ed., by William Strunk, Jr., E. B. White, Roger Angell (Longman, 2000). Originally written in 1918 by William Strunk, Jr., and then revised and expanded in 1959 by E. B. White and later by Roger Angell, this slim 105-page volume has a wealth of information on how to write so you're understood.

✳ *Lapsing into a Comma*, by Bill Walsh (McGraw-Hill, 2000). This "curmudgeon's guide to the many things that can go wrong in print—and how to avoid them" is great fun to read and enormously helpful when you're puzzled.

✳ *On Writing Well*, 25th anniversary ed., by William Zinsser (HarperResource, 2001). This timeless volume will help you clear up fuzzy thinking, cluttered sentences, passive verbs, and a host of other writing patterns we all fall into if we're not keeping a sharp eye on what we're doing.

✳ Poetry (poetry.com). Nothing rhymes with *orange*, but if there's a poet in your soul struggling to get out, you'll appreciate this website, which gives you more than just a rhyming dictionary. Find poems, contests, evaluations, and more—it's a one-stop shop where you can rhyme till you drop.

* *The Write Way*, by Richard Lederer and Richard Dowis (Pocket Books, 1995). Almost anything by Richard Lederer is great fun and highly instructive, and this guide to "Real-Life Writing" is no exception. Lederer is a linguist who thoroughly enjoys the language with all its strengths, weaknesses, and oddities.

CHAPTER 9:

Internet English

* Babel Fish Translation (http://babelfish.altavista.com). If you want to test a translation—or see how your Internet message will look in another language—this is a perfect place to try it out. You can translate up to a 150-word block of text from English to twelve languages and from each of these languages back to English. A world keyboard allows you to enter accented words or Cyrillic characters.

* Wordtracker (wordtracker.com). Wordtracker can help you make your website come up in Google searches. It shows you which are the most popular keywords and then how to use them in your Web copy.

* yourDictionary.com (yourdictionary.com). How do you say hello in Hindi? Find out here. This site links to online dictionaries that translate English into more than three hundred languages, and vice versa. It has a world of information on English words, too.

CHAPTER 10:

Regionalspeak

* Global Language Monitor (languagemonitor.com). Claiming to be the largest overseer of global English usage, this site tracks the language around the world. It's a fascinating resource, but be careful—this is another one where you could easily spend more time than you originally intended.

* Slanguage (slanguage.com). This fun, if not academically accurate, site lists slang city by city all over the world. Slang terms are submitted by natives, not by linguists, and there is a section on teen slang.

INDEX